THE SOUL OF DESIGN

THE SOUL OF DESIGN

*Harnessing the Power of Plot to
Create Extraordinary Products*

Lee Devin and Robert D. Austin

STANFORD BUSINESS BOOKS
An Imprint of Stanford University Press
Stanford, California

Stanford University Press
Stanford, California

Special discounts for bulk quantities of Stanford Business Books
are available to corporations, professional associations, and other
organizations. For details and discount information, contact the special
sales department of Stanford University Press. Tel: (650) 736-1782,
Fax: (650) 736-1784

Printed in the United States of America on acid-free, archival-quality paper

Library of Congress Cataloging-in-Publication Data

Devin, Lee, 1938- author.
  The soul of design : harnessing the power of plot to create extraordinary
products / Lee Devin and Robert D. Austin.
      pages cm
  Includes bibliographical references and index.
  ISBN 978-0-8047-5720-1 (alk. paper)
  1. Product design. 2. New products—Management. 3. Product
management. I. Austin, Robert D. (Robert Daniel), 1962– author. II. Title.

TS171.4.D497 2012

658.5'752—dc23

                        2012009561

Typeset by Classic Typography in 11.25/16 Sabon MT Pro

The poet or maker should be the maker of
plots rather than of verses. . . .

—ARISTOTLE, *POETICS*, PART IX

CONTENTS

ACKNOWLEDGMENTS

WE GRATEFULLY ACKNOWLEDGE the support of the dean and Division of Research at Harvard Business School, the president of Copenhagen Business School, and the president of Swarthmore College, without which we could not have accomplished the research involved in this project. We are also indebted to the many people and organizations, named and unnamed in this book, who generously gave of their time to help us prepare research and teaching case studies. We thank also the students, by now in excess of a thousand, who have offered in class their thoughts and reactions to the teaching cases produced on the way to this book; these discussions in class with students have resulted in very real contributions to this work.

We are happy in friends and colleagues who have been of great help as this book developed. These include the following.

For Lee: Lyssa Adkins, Marcia Brown, Sandra Devin, Sean Devin, Siobhan Devin, Charles Gilbert, Donald Kent, Ryan Martens, Tobias Mayer, David Mooberry, Shannon O'Donnell, Geoff Proehl, Steve Salter, David Smith, Eleanor Smith, Michael Spayd, Jean Tabaka, Preston Trombley, Stacia Viscardi, and Gordon Wickstrom.

Generations of students at Swarthmore College who, in the student-teacher exchange, gave as good as they got.

Colleagues and friends at People's Light and Theatre: actors and directors I taught, learned from, rehearsed with, and watched with awe (and envy) over the years.

In a class by herself: advisor, enabler, deep companion, beloved wife, Abigail Adams.

For Rob: Colleagues at Harvard Business School, then Copenhagen Business School, then the Faculty of Business Administration at the University of New Brunswick Fredericton, who provided encouragement and feedback throughout the writing of this book. Anna Ward and the other members of the Dean's Office staff at UNBF, who worked hard to help with the preparation of the manuscript (and oh so much else).

Family: Laurel, Lillian, Evelyn, and Daniel Austin, who supported me in so many ways during the writing; and my parents, Sylvia and Bob Austin, who have made all things possible over the years—my father, the original Robert Austin, departed from us this year, and is greatly missed every day in many ways.

Also dear and departed, and due great thanks for his help with this work: José Royo, former CEO of Ascent Media Group (Ascent was a case study), a former student and one of the greatest talents ever to emerge from the Harvard Business School, who left this earth far too soon at the tender age of forty-four. Others we must thank: anonymous reviewers of the manuscript, as well as those who were (eventually) not anonymous, Ruth Beresen, Fred Collopy, Rasmus Bech Hansen, and Rafael Ramirez.

Our patient, dauntless editor, Margo Beth Fleming, amazing copyeditor, David Horne, and the others at Stanford University Press with whom we've had the good fortune to work.

For the book as a whole: Hank Murta Adams, James Barker, Ed Catmull, Frank Coker, Arthur De Vaney, Lucinda Duncalfe,

Jette Egelund, Kasper Egelund, Sofie Egelund, Jonas Hecksher, Rasmus Ibfelt, David Lewis, Shannon O'Donnell, Fred Orthlieb, Søren Overgaard, Flemming Møller Pedersen, Ptolemy, Matthew Reckard, Jonathan Roberts, Paul Robertson, Paul Ulrik Skifter, Bill Soloman, Thorkil Sonne, Torben Ballegaard Sørensen, and Erin Sullivan.

The problem with making a list is that you always leave someone off it. Thanks too, then, to those whom we should have listed here but whom we've left off due to inexcusable oversight.

Lee Devin—Swarthmore, Pennsylvania, USA
Robert D. Austin—Fredericton, New Brunswick, Canada

THE SOUL OF DESIGN

PART ONE

NON-ORDINARY PRODUCTS

(AND SERVICES)

I

An elegant woman, slight of stature, apparently in her fifties, stands at the front of a class listening as a twenty-three-year-old poses a question that's actually a veiled criticism. Responding, the woman repeats something she said earlier. She struggles with a remote control, moving back through four or five PowerPoint slides to show something she's shown before. She apologizes for her English, which is in fact eloquent. When she chooses an un-usual word, or constructs a sentence oddly, you recognize a bet-ter expression of her ideas than anything you thought she might say. But some in the room don't hear the poetry, or it doesn't persuade them. A murmur ripples through the crowd as young people shift in their chairs.

Jette Egelund, chair of a company called "Vipp," has accepted an invitation to lecture to "Managing in the Creative Economy," a class at the Copenhagen Business School, about her experiences growing the company. But now the students—some of them— have begun to lecture *her*. They hasten to offer Ms. Egelund *their* wisdom, gained from instruction in business school as well as from their twenty-something experiences. She listens politely, but she's got fire in her eye and steel in her backbone.

In a way, she's invited this onslaught: she's told the class that she, unlike them, has no training in business. She's told stories that profess an innocence of conventional business logic (actually, a reluctance to accept it, but the students don't notice that). She's disagreed with the students on such questions as whether she ought to think about customers in distinct segments (she prefers not to). She's spoken proudly of introducing products that, according to conventional business wisdom, should never have been launched (although these products have been successful); of disregarding customer feedback in order to pursue personal notions of design integrity in her products (although this practice doesn't seem to have prevented their success). She professes ignorance on important topics and, disturbingly, appears pleased about this. The students' questions have a subtext: it's only a matter of time before such commercial misbehavior will catch up with her. One student finally says it out loud, not bothering to disguise his opinion as a question.

Vipp sells "designer" trashcans and toilet brushes. The bin (trashcan) is the company's iconic product (Figure 1.1). It's featured in the collections of design museums. It's been on display at the Louvre. The very idea of a museum-worthy designer trashcan or toilet brush raises eyebrows.

But customers appreciate these products. And they pay high prices for them. The floor-standing 30-liter Vipp 24 bin, for example, sells for €350 or $400 or even $500, depending on the market. The company's celebrated toilet brush sells for €129, or more than $200 in some markets. These price points, in combination with the firm's rapid growth rate,[1] constitute a business triumph. Most people think about trash cans and toilet brushes

FIGURE I.I. Vipp 16 Bin.
Source: Vipp, reprinted by permission.

in purely functional terms, but functionality alone can't justify
these prices. Vipp products function well, but not *that* well.
Product profit margins are, well, *huge*.[2]

Jette's father, Holger, made the first Vipp bin in 1939, and
the bin itself, the physical object, hasn't changed much since. In
those days the bins sold in modest volumes, at modest prices.
Not until Jette took over, in the early 1990s, did the firm begin
to grow. Holger, an artful soul who loved ballroom dancing,
could not delegate, and thus never expanded the business beyond
a few employees. Production-oriented and practical, he never
imagined the bin as anything other than a better-than-average
refuse receptacle. He priced it by estimating production cost and
adding a small percentage. When Jette, forced to take over the
company after her father died, looked at the bin, however, she
experienced much more than a functional relationship with a
reliable garbage can.

She saw the story of her parents, Holger and Marie, a young
couple struggling to make a life together in the years just before
and during the Second World War. She saw a stylish home fur-
nishing, a finely designed and sculpted form that reflected her

father's aesthetic sensibilities. She saw a beautiful object worthy of placement in a museum, a thing that she'd lived with all her life, and that she had, with her own hands, made, again and again at her father's side. This bin, in her eyes, in her memory and imagination, seemed *special*.

In the years since, she has made it special for others as well. In 2006, Vipp bins decorated or reconceived by famous designers filled the windows of Copenhagen's posh department store, Det Ny Illum, alongside arrangements of clothing and accessories by Armani, Prada, and Donna Karan. A few months later, the Louvre displayed ornamented Vipp bins as *objets d'art*. By 2009, Ms. Egelund no longer made bins with her own hands, but she gently broadcast the confident authority of someone who knew her business in every detail—even when confronted by twenty-something B-school hotshots.

Standing before that group, she explains her novel conception, an idea more expansive and interesting than will fit into these students' broad mental boxes. The issue of the bin's qualities comes to a head when a student offers a conjecture: if Vipp becomes *too* successful, he says, if the company sells *too many* bins, it will become difficult to keep prices high. When everyone has a bin, he opines, the product will lose its cachet; it won't set the owner of a Vipp bin apart from other people.

Ms. Egelund answers simply, "Do you think so?" Then she explains (again!) why she thinks people buy the bin: They like it. They find it beautiful. The student thinks she misunderstands and repeats the question. Ms. Egelund shrugs and disagrees with his premise. She does not think there is danger in the Vipp bin being everywhere because, as she puts it, "I have looked at it my entire life, and I still quite enjoy looking at it." She speaks briefly of the Vipp toilet brush, opposed by many but selling well. She rejects the student's assumption that the bin appeals only to customer snobbery. Even in the most crowded market, she counters, there's always room for something that people "quite like to look at." Or listen to. Or experience in some other way. What sets such a thing apart, according to Jette Egelund, is not how many other people have the thing, or how well they can use it to show off their money or good taste, but something internal to the thing itself.

In a different class about Vipp on another day we were startled to hear from a young college student on a tight budget that she owned *five* Vipp bins. Why, we asked, do you own five? Do you even have five rooms in your apartment? No, she confessed, she did not have five rooms, and did not really need five bins. "But," she explained, "I just *love* them. There's something about them that I appreciate."

What is that something? And how does it get in there?

These are central questions in this book.

2

A Bang & Olufsen TV sells for four to five times the price of a functionally comparable Sony. And the price on a B&O TV stays high a long time; typically, the price of a model goes up when the company discontinues it. Apple products, from iPads to MacBooks, sell for higher prices and in higher volumes than comparably equipped competing products. Sales of the iPad reached one million units in twenty-eight days. Something makes other products special, too, products from Alessi, Artemide, BMW, Bodum, Caravaggio, Custo Barcelona, Decathalon, Droog, Ducati, Eva Solo, Ferrari, Fredericia, Fritz Hansen, Frog Design, Gubi, and so on. An understanding of innovation based purely on technological improvement or functionality—and as far as we can tell, this describes much of the current management research on the subject—doesn't get us to these products, can't explain their appeal, and won't point managers toward certain useful competitive strategies. The conventional research on technological innovation and product development won't lead you to a sixty-year-old trash bin design that sells for $500 or an Mp3 player that sells two hundred million units at considerably better profit margins than the functionally similar competition.[3]

Not all companies can do this. Not too long ago, Walmart—one of the biggest and richest companies on earth, able to summon any marketing company in the world to its Bentonville, Arkansas, headquarters—began to experiment with making products more special. It created "Metro 7" (fashionable women's clothing), "George" (fashionable men's clothing), and "Exsto" (fashionable and organic children's clothing).[4] These lines featured slightly higher prices than Walmart ordinarily charged for clothing, and they aimed at higher product profit margins, though still modest compared with Vipp or Apple. But Walmart's efforts didn't go well. Consumers rejected the company's attempts to move "upscale." *BusinessWeek*, in a cover story, pointed to the firm's difficulties as evidence of a mid-life crisis.[5] Lee Scott, the Walmart CEO, gave *BusinessWeek* his own interpretation of the company's difficulties: "We can't wake up one morning and say we're going to be something different . . . and not earn it."[6]

3

Beautiful. Elegant. Exciting. Cool. People use these and similar words when they encounter something they consider special. Such words express reactions to a thing more than they describe the thing itself. We substitute *reaction* for *description* partly because what's within the thing that provokes the reaction is difficult to grasp and describe. It's not merely a matter of appearance. It's also not a matter of simple emotional response. Your reflexive attraction to a thing—a Big Mac when you're really hungry, say—does not make that thing special. Special things generate feelings, but so do many annoying things: the dog's accident on the carpet, for instance. We're also not talking about pleasure only; special products provoke a range of responses, some not immediately pleasant at all.

To get at what's within a special thing, that which makes it special, then, it appears we'll need to set aside personal taste and individual response. We'll need to adopt a more technical, more abstract consideration. In our explorations within these pages, we'll try out a number of ideas about this, but we'll start with an internal view. We will, at first, treat our subjects—those special things—as independent of conditions outside themselves. That's not easy to do, and it will take a lot more explaining. But it's worth the effort.

4

We're meditating upon a mystery here, the uncanny power of some products to grab and hold attention, to create desire. We won't claim to have solved this mystery, and we certainly won't suggest reducing it to a set of step-by-step instructions. Far from it. This book won't "prove" anything. Formally, our research approach has been constructed to generate and explore possible ideas, not to solve, reduce, or prove anything. We'll propose an idea (or two) for you to try on. Maybe you'll find that helpful. We offer a way to think sensibly enough, and clearly enough, that you can become "comfortable" in the ambiguity of the mystery's secret, and okay with your inability to penetrate that secret completely. We'll try to get you closer, but you'll have to take yourself the rest of the way as it applies to your situation, your business. We intend to celebrate rather than analyze the mystery. It is, after all, what makes special things special.

5

We have a simple mission in this book: we intend, as carefully and thoughtfully as we can, to explore Jette Egelund's hypothesis that there is something within a special thing that makes it special, and that changes the way you should think about making and marketing it. Our idea—the basic idea that we suggest you try on, even if it seems like a stretch at first—is that a special thing exhibits the quality of *well-constructed plot*. It's good *plot* that's in there, that's the source of exclaimed reactions, that's at the heart of Ms. Egelund's convictions. We need to say a lot more about what we mean by *plot*, by *well-constructed*, and much else, but bear with us while we finish laying out the idea.

When a thing displays well-constructed plot that is *coherent*, we'll refer to it as *non-ordinary*. Plotted coherently, the interactive parts of a non-ordinary thing together generate *resonance*, an enhancement of power that causes a thing to become greater and more effective than the sum of its parts would predict. Resonance incites reactions from people. It's those reactions that cause people to experience a thing as *special*. And it's those reactions that can lead to commercial success (revenues, profits). The likelihood that a coherent (non-ordinary) thing will generate powerful reactions and commercial success (and thus be considered special) depends, to large but not total extent, on how well a company addresses certain challenges inherent in plotting and making a thing's unique coherence accessible to its audience or customers.

To sum up: a maker plots a structure to achieve coherence; coherence supposes an interaction among parts that generates resonance. We call such things non-ordinary. Resonance, a quality of a coherently plotted non-ordinary thing, incites reactions from people. And it's those reactions that cause people to experience a non-ordinary thing as *special*.

That's it. That's the idea we'd like you to consider.

We still have work to do, of course, to explain it in a way that will provide helpful insights. We'll have to take on the major job of explaining what *plot* means for an object in space, like a TV or an iPad. Most people are accustomed to thinking about plot in books, movies, or plays. We'll start with these familiar notions of plot before moving to the more abstract and more challenging idea. But extending the idea to objects in space presents no insurmountable problem, as you will soon see, and it leaves us with a powerful toolkit for thinking about special things.

In the course of reflecting on what we've called non-ordinary things, we'll invoke their strange attraction and describe their *self-referential construction*. To do this we won't list features, narrate making processes, or promulgate rules. Instead, we'll gather and reflect on some ideas common to the men and women in our research sample. And we'll make copious use of examples. We intend our examples to show not what some artist or maker did so that you can repeat it, but how the main features of a special thing fit together and how a maker at a particular place and time did that fitting. What we learned in the research, and our descriptions of how that learning applies to non-ordinary products and services, will combine, we hope, in your imagination to create your own unique sensitivity to special things. We seek to present both data and meditations on data that will construct an "idea" of non-ordinary products.

We use that term, *idea*, in a sort of Platonic sense: We invite you to imagine the perfect idea of the extraordinary product. The idea you derive from our meditation won't appear in the world. It will instead apply to all such products and will often exhibit mutually exclusive features. For instance, when we consider magnitude, a thing's proper size, we'll suggest that a non-ordinary product should be as large and/or complicated as possible, but at the same time small and/or simple enough to be apprehended and experienced. There's no rule about percentages of big and little, simple and complex; we have an *idea* of proper magnitude.

Our hope that you'll create your own guiding idea leads us to use examples as our principle method of staging ideas, and to use a number of examples taken from art, often from theater, work we feel comfortable with and in which the notion of "plot" comes naturally. Works of art create a distance between themselves and the "real" world. It's counterintuitive at first to treat an iPod as a thing complete in itself and independent of function. It's possible, but an understanding of its function and a personal taste in gadgets will interfere. A work of art has a purity here that a useful gadget doesn't.

In short, we'll ask you to set aside some of your industrially conditioned ideas and attitudes about making and selling. Special things don't thrive in the industrial frame of mind that has been so successful in business up to now. They need to be made and sold differently. The aesthetic frame of mind we ask you to explore isn't a dumbing down or a lack of precision. Artists are among the most hardheaded and precise people we know. But they see synthetically, not analytically; they see the path, not the gravel.

And they can do creative work on a schedule. No business deadline is as inflexible as opening night. That launch can't be postponed.[7] So we urge you to leave at the door your false preconceptions, your stereotypes of artists starving in a garret, and join us as we meander through a landscape on a journey that leads to better understanding of the nature of special things and the people and businesses that make and sell them.[8]

6

This book is ultimately about how to manage creative companies. But we'll have to work up to that. At its heart is a notion of what makes a special thing special, and we'll have to deal with that first. The thoughts we have about how to manage creative processes and companies derive specifically from our core ideas about the non-ordinary structure of special products and services. We won't deal with every aspect of how to run a creative

NON-ORDINARY PRODUCTS (AND SERVICES)   11

business, just those implied by our explanation of non-ordinary things and how they obtain effects.

This is no small matter, however. Our ideas about what makes products and services special lead to some pretty unconventional management practices. If you take into account what we're saying about special things, you won't manage the way you might have been taught in business school, or the way you learned to manage a factory, an insurance company, or one of many other businesses. We're on the hunt for insights into how to lead creative businesses; we're looking at the things those businesses make in a particular way. To start down this path, we'll need to look more closely at what we mean by *plot*, in a context in which the word seems natural.

7

Plot calls to mind story, because the most obvious evidence of plotting is the sequence of events in a story. We use the word differently, as a term of art. It's important to notice that those story events are almost never arranged in simple chronology. As soon as the story gets the least bit complicated, arrangements must be made: "Meanwhile, back at the ranch. . . . " The decision about where to put this or that incident; the relationships among incidents and other features—that's plotting. Reactions to a special thing occur in space as well as time. The idea, plot, conceived as a quality, can help you organize the arrangements made by a maker.

The Sixth Sense, a movie written and directed by M. Night Shyamalan, did well at the box office and with the critics. Its major star, Bruce Willis, gained it a start on 2,161 screens in the United States, a good-sized opening but not huge. Over the next six weeks, more theaters picked it up, as it became clear that this film "had legs"; audiences liked it. Eventually, the movie's run extended to thirty-nine weeks, a rather long time in the biz. It won six Academy Award and four BAFTA (British Oscar) nominations, and two People's Choice awards.

Our interest in *The Sixth Sense*, however, is not in proclaiming its artistic merits (though we don't dispute those). We single it out for its quality of plot. The way the maker plots the story he tells, how he creates patterns and arranges trajectories, is not at all subtle. Plot, the way its parts go together, is this film's most prominent feature. And that's an advantage to us as we look at how a maker creates a unique form.

As the movie begins, Dr. Malcolm Crowe, a child psychologist, has just received a prestigious award; he's home with his wife, Anna, after the ceremony. They're celebrating. Their conversation includes information: he's sacrificed a lot for his work, putting everything else second. ("Including," Anna says, "me.") The two enjoy a moment of triumph in their tastefully decorated Philadelphia townhouse. They share an old and expensive wine (an early image shows Anna, in their wine cellar, selecting the bottle).

But watch them celebrate. Remember the ominous music of the opening. This movie is a thriller. Remember that Anna thought she heard something as she picked out that bottle of wine. All the celebrating and self-congratulating seems destined for interruption. Knowledge of movie conventions kicks in: a trajectory, composed of recognizable patterns that range from "too much celebrating" ("Hubris!") to a creepy camera placement on a shot of Anna in the basement ("There's someone behind you!"), points to a likelihood that an intruder has sneaked into the house. Shyamalan fulfills this expectation. As the couple moves upstairs, to the bedroom, Anna discovers a broken window; soon after, they find a weeping, nearly naked young man in the bathroom. Unpleasantness ensues. This sequence contains material both generally familiar (ominous music, broken window) and specifically surprising (nearly naked intruder). Shyamalan will repeat and develop these materials throughout the movie, plotting the shape of an emerging form. He'll create expectations and then present the actual form he has chosen, eventually leading to a startling reversal and closure.

8

Our approach to special things, our attempt to understand the soul of *design*, owes a big debt to Aristotle. For our money, his ideas about how the form of a thing consists of interdependent, coherently arranged parts have never been eclipsed. Bear in mind that Aristotle had no idea of modern mass production; for him, any made thing was unique, one of a kind. He wrote an important book about making, commonly called *Poetics*. He used for his main example a very complicated made thing he'd studied closely and knew well, a kind of play called tragedy. Greek cities put tragedies at the center of their combination religious, civic, and business festivals. Scholars have mostly translated the full title of his *Ars Poetica* as *On the Art of Poetry*. But Kenneth Telford, one of his best translators, suggests that *Concerning the Productive* might be better, or *Concerning Productive Science*.[9] Aristotle's ideas about how things become what they are, the qualities and parts common to all made things, and much else, can help us to think precisely about making special products and services, things that cannot be compared to other things and must be judged on their own terms.[10]

Aristotle called plot "the soul of tragedy."[11] For him, this soul was the major animating principle that organized the parts of each individual script into a unique example of the class of things called tragedy. It labels the *principle of organization* that creates the self-referential structure of special things. We borrow *plot* from Aristotle's *Poetics* to use it in this exact sense. We need the word, the idea, in order to approach an understanding of the complex interaction of parts in a special thing.

9

Think of *coherence* as the aim of plotting. Plot exhibits as the coherence of a thing while it unfolds in time and space. People engage with that emerging "shape" and they experience, usually not completely consciously, its unified wholeness. The feelings we experience when we encounter a special thing arise from an experience of form, often from the sense of surprise people feel when they recognize that the form of an emergent thing is better (more attractive or more useful, say) than the expected or familiar.

There's an apparent contradiction here. People get strong feelings when they encounter a special thing. At a museum, sit in front of a painting as other people have been doing for several hundred years. You know the painter couldn't have put his attention on *you* all those years ago. But you feel a connection. The painter made this connection when he put his attention on the form he was making, plotting its myriad parts into a coherent structure for the maximum resonance among those interdependent parts. That's the painting's affect, what you feel in response to an encounter with form.

A special thing's coherent form begins with *patterns* (Figure 1.2). These are hooks, basic component shapes that people recognize; a collection of lines, shapes, and symbols that evoke

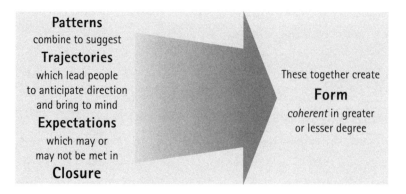

Patterns
combine to suggest
Trajectories
which lead people
to anticipate direction
and bring to mind
Expectations
which may or
may not be met in
Closure

These together create
Form
coherent in greater
or lesser degree

FIGURE 1.2. The Creation of Form.

from shared cultural conventions a more complex idea. Lines in a drawing by Durer might lead you to recognize a "hand"; lines and symbols in a newspaper might lead you to recognize "a falling stock market." A special thing includes many patterns arranged in relation to each other, whether primarily in space or in time. Placed together, plotted, these patterns suggest *trajectories* toward further possible outcomes. They encourage you to *anticipate* developments. Sometimes you anticipate what does happen, sometimes you don't.

It's a natural, universal human reflex to anticipate the future of a pattern, to extend trajectories from collections of patterns. We *experience* form when we perceive and expect, when we check our expectations against the actual "shape" the maker composed. Eventually, in a coherent form, the shape achieves a *closure* that brings all of its parts together. Often this closure will surprise us; the form that we perceive is not what we anticipated but something better. A person will naturally feel affect, perhaps even strong emotion, during this experience of the relationships among anticipation, realization, and closure.

But this feeling, though caused by the form's coherence, is not the test of its coherence. Coherence is an *intrinsic* quality of the made thing. It can cause external effects, but the effects are a result of coherence, not coherence itself. And, as you'll see, coherence of form does not guarantee favorable external effects. Not all great products or services or works of art gain commercial appreciation. We'll have much more to say on this point later.

10

Resonance is what we call the enhancement of a thing's powers that results from well-constructed—coherent—form. A thing becomes greater than the sum of its parts because of the way those parts interact and resonate with each other. In physics, resonance means the reinforcement or prolongation of sound by reflection from a surface or by the synchronous vibration of a neighboring object. In a violin, say, the sound of vibrating strings creates resonances in the shaped woods of the instrument's body. The differences in sound between the fiddle that a child brings home from school and the Domenico Montagnana made in Venice in 1729 and played by Paul Robertson in the Medici Quartet (one of our case subjects), lie in qualities of the woods—their thicknesses, densities, and shapes; in the size and shape of the holes cut into some parts of it—the curves and stresses carved and bent into the wood; and in the varnishes that preserve it and contribute to the varying densities. All these "parts" of the Montagnana act on each other, with each other; in resonance they create the astonishing sounds Robertson can cause by scraping some sticky horsehair across a tight string. A child's machine-made instrument can't compare. The interdependent parts of a made thing, plotted into coherence, create a mysterious jump, the ineffable quality we've called resonance.

Resonance is a convenient metaphor to evoke the mysterious power of the products we've called special. You've probably participated in or observed an exceptional team that "somehow" comes together, clicks, and makes conceptual leaps that none of its members could make on their own. Team members will talk about being together in unusual ways, of close communication, of collaboration, but mostly they'll rely on "feeling words" to *evoke* rather than describe or define their experience.

II

This resonance, a result of a product's plotted coherence, resembles the same effect in a work of art. This means that we can think about non-ordinary products with ideas that people have developed about art. Interdependence of parts distinguishes *objets d'art* from ordinary objects. You can see this when you look at a painting made long ago—Rembrandt's portraits, for instance. In spite of their different clothing, and the settings in which they appear, these characters might be people you know, contemporaries. Rembrandt didn't paint them so that you'd recognize them three hundred fifty years later or so that the colors would complement your new sofa. He painted parts (lines, shapes, colors) that *relate to and refer to each other*, not to the world outside the picture. Looking at such paintings you can think about them unfettered by limitations of past ideas or future desires. Special things invite this freedom of contemplation. This is important for innovation processes as they approach closure.

12

We need to be up front with some potentially controversial implications of what we're proposing here. Non-ordinary products are special, we're suggesting, because they have a form with certain qualities that we can describe and discuss. Non-ordinary products have their significance, not because of their effect on people, but because they have a coherent form that produces resonance. Think of resonance, this human reaction to coherence, however you wish, as an awakening of sensitivity or as neurons firing energetically; however you conceive it, realize that we propose *form* as the determining feature of objects, services, and experiences made non-ordinary. Reactions to a special thing issue in response to that form, and are external to it. They are not part of nor are they evidence of *soul* in the thing. The form excites, it does not contain or express. The feelings that lead us to words such as *beautiful* or *cool* or *elegant* or *meaningful*, though of course important, are a derivative consequence and not an essential part of the self-referential qualities that make the form unique.[12]

We're making a big deal of this partly because it constitutes a distinctly different approach from that taken by much research in the sociology of art. Sociologists, not surprisingly, envision art at the center of social processes that support its production, legitimize certain products (or de-legitimize others), and lead to commerce. Some of them back away from the idea that aesthetic worth derives from intrinsic qualities of a special thing. They suggest instead that regard for special things is *socially constructed.*

13

Saying that non-ordinary products have coherent forms in no way means they have the *same* form, or that they are formulaic. A maker plots coherence for each unique made thing. The principle expresses itself in the materials, constructive energy, and form of each thing; as each is unique, so the expression is unique. Understanding what makes things you already know about special can help you make choices about a new product, but coherence doesn't reduce to a spec sheet: it's a quality, not a set of instructions. Every special thing is unique, special for its own reasons, and that means the maker has to work out every new one anew. There are no shortcuts. To arrive at something special, you must begin at the beginning, every time. You must do the work just as artists do theirs: as if for the very first time.

Of course special things can be copied, manufactured, put in a box. There are many identical Vipp bins, many iPads, and many reproductions of works by Picasso. Copying special things is a different matter from making new ones. Perhaps this is a pretty obvious point, but we need to be clear about it.

14

Because this is a book about business, about creating commercial value, we can't focus alone on matters of internal form; we can't leave out the relations things have outside themselves. We need to see a special thing in two main ways, to exercise a kind of doublethink. A special thing is a stand-alone thing, made of interdependent parts and free of "meaning" or "usefulness."[13] It's also a commercial product that has market potential.

In the first case, the thing is made the way it is solely to be the way it is. Its final purpose is to be perfect of its kind. This useful tautology asserts that some things, like works of art, must be judged on intrinsic principles and not in comparison to other, perhaps superficially similar, things. The tautology's counterintuitive oddness will help remind you of the difference between ordinary and special and also help you maintain the imaginative discipline necessary to conceive a single object in two different ways.

In the second way of seeing special things, we conceive the thing as made for a purpose beyond completion of its own form: to create commercial value. As a new product emerges from the processes of its making, managers, designers, and other makers must consider its potential as a commercial product and speculate on its power to create commercial value. This second purpose extends away from the thing itself and into the world of marketing, managing, and functioning.

To profit from non-ordinary products requires then a certain mental discipline: you're trying to succeed commercially, in extrinsic terms. But to do that, *you need to focus on creating a thing that you judge on its intrinsic qualities* (resonant coherence). Note that this is an *idea*. It's a method. A concept. In everyday life, of course, any thing exists in a context of relationships with things outside itself. But to make judgments about closure when making a new thing, for instance, you must be able to clear your mind of limitations caused by your desire that the thing be a success in the market.

How can that help us create business value with non-ordinary products? Simply put, business needs some language and thinking on which to build theories and methodologies for considering, making, judging, improving, managing, and marketing new, non-ordinary, and thus unique products. A thing of which there is only one resists efforts to compare, contrast, and classify. It stands alone. There are plenty of paintings of smiling women; each is unique. You can compare your responses to them, and you can compare the plotting of their parts. But each remains only itself. So in these reflections, we want to make a specific, narrow use of some aesthetic language and ideas to address products that cause feelings that no one can describe or even name. These three core ideas—plot, coherence, and resonance—when applied to business products, services, teams, workspace, and management practice are sufficiently strange to make their technical use possible without much overlap from everyday terms.

Language is a tool people use to think with. We need the best tools we can find or invent to approach what we see as an increasingly important field in business: the need for innovation, and for ways to address that need without undue reliance on guesswork or sterile industrial methods. We've written elsewhere about the economic forces that are creating a gradual shift in the United States from industrial replication of physical things (manufacturing) to artful making of unique things (ideas, innovations).[14]

15

What accounts for the way customers respond to, think about, and experience non-ordinary products? How do such things influence business competition? To arrive at answers to these and similar questions, we have for the past several years studied makers (people, groups, and companies) in fields from the arts to aerospace, from graphic design to media, and from consumer electronics to pharmaceuticals. The background for this book is a rigorously crafted *grounded theory* research project.

A grounded theory project is, by its nature, *inductive*; it seeks to reason from specifics—case studies of makers—to general principles. Such an approach is a great route to constructing new frameworks, general ideas and language to use to describe an observed phenomenon. Such a research approach is, however, incapable of arriving at proof of a general claim. Doing that requires a different kind of research. In the way research programs usually progress, inductive research generates possible explanations, which *deductive* research then tests. We're doing only the former, coming up with new explanations, not proving them. This is why we've taken a somewhat tentative approach in this book.

You should know, however, that we've done a great deal of careful research in support of what we write here. We examined a total of thirty detailed case studies (there's a full list of them at the back of the book), most of them conducted by a dedicated team of half a dozen researchers. We made site visits across countries and continents over a span of several years. We video taped hundreds of hours of interviews and carefully analyzed them within each case and across cases. We followed that with many more hours of "coding" in accord with protocols for analysis refined to avoid bias. Thousands of pages of "case treatments" that organize observations and interview responses into a framework emerged from the project as it went along. We also had hundreds of hours of conversation to define and describe boundaries of the processes we studied, to refine our analysis approach, and to reconcile differences of points of view into something we could all believe in on the basis of evidence.[15]

All the people and groups in our cases make things, but they don't all make non-ordinary things. We chose cases that range across a variety of conditions, and across this range from ordinary to non-ordinary. Comparing making of ordinary and non-ordinary allows us to understand what's different about the latter.

Fourteen of our case subjects are individual artists. Artists work in ways we could easily observe; we could watch the creation of a new metal sculpture from start to finish; we couldn't do that for the creation of a new drug. Our movement back and forth between small-scale (for example, metal sculpture) and large-scale (such as drug development) settings generated rich comparisons. Observations of the former helped us to reach insightful interpretations of the latter.

It would be wrong to suppose that art cases clustered only with other art cases and business cases clustered only with other business cases in our analyses. Often we found that ways of working in some businesses resembled ways of working in artistic organizations, that some businesses resembled artists more than they resembled other businesses, and vice versa for artists. Thus a capital-intensive manufacturing operation worked in ways surprisingly similar to those of a team mounting a replication of a Broadway musical. Both saw their job as using diverse inputs to produce an outcome as nearly identical as possible to an output specification. The manufacturing operation wanted to hit its quality targets, whereas the Broadway musical company aspired to a production as close to the New York production as possible, to "protect the brand." Both teams aimed at replication; thus neither intended to produce new non-ordinary outcomes, even though one might be considered an artist. Other art and business pairs clustered together and resembled each other because they were trying to produce new non-ordinary outcomes.

This extensive process, of case-based comparison and analysis, has led us to a view of what makes some products special and how that might help create business value. Even more important, it has given us a way to look into how people confront and exploit the challenges of plot and soul within their products, services, and businesses.

16

We organized this book into five parts. In Part 1, this part, we have introduced the idea of plot in experiences of products and services, and also the notion of its impacts on commercial outcomes. In Part 2, we examine plot, and the parts that plotting arranges in time and space. In Part 3, we describe the formal qualities of plot—the features that make for coherent plotting—and we connect coherence to resonance, pointing out that the connection is far from certain—coherence can generate resonance, but it does not always. In Part 4, we describe the challenges of making sure coherence results from making, especially in business contexts, and the further challenges of making coherent forms accessible to an audience or customers so that they can experience resonance. It's in this part that we draw most heavily on our detailed casework, which shows how makers managed the challenges of ensuring coherence in and resonance from special things. Finally, in the short Part 5, we wrap up and summarize.

17

Once, when we presented the Vipp story at a Harvard Business School alumni event, a marketing consultant emerged from the audience to say, "I do this all the time, and I can do it with any trash can." She meant she could, through clever marketing, get people to consider anything as special.

We doubt it. Of course there's skillful marketing and PR involved with Vipp bins, iPads, and B&O TVs. New things need savvy (well plotted) introduction into existing markets, so that their intrinsic, self-referential excellence can translate into success as measured by external, commercial criteria such as sales and profits. To make value from a special thing, you must have customers, and marketing can teach customers how to engage with unique (and therefore strange) things offered for sale.

But coherent plotting cannot be added on to just any trashcan. Plot *is* the trashcan. Nor can resonance be found absent coherence. Some products have a differentiating aura that arises only when the products and their surrounding materials and activities (such as marketing and sales) relate to each other in an aesthetically coherent manner. Features that we usually label "marketing" or "PR" are, for such products, plotted into relationships with the thing itself in ways that create a coherent whole. Consequently, these products *have resonance* for the people who buy them. Step into an Apple store, or the Vipp display at a department store. The product's designed surroundings are a part of what it *is*, part of what customers learn about and take delight in, not something external to it. What you know about such products, what the makers have caused you to know, and how they have caused you to know it all condition your responses and provide the experience you need to become a customer.

18

Torben Ballegaard Sørensen, a former CEO of Bang & Olufsen, told us about a disagreement he had with designer David Lewis when the company ran out of a crucial component for a popular TV model in the lead-up to the Christmas season. To accommodate an available substitute component, engineers needed to add two centimeters depth to the back of a large TV. In four meetings with the designer, the CEO heard again and again, "This will spoil the whole thing." In the end, Lewis redesigned the overall shape of the TV so that the extra two centimeters would not spoil the whole thing. Sørensen observed,

Good designers are strong personalities. They are dangerous because they can walk out on a cliff if they think that's what they should do, but they are valuable because of their own strong interpretation of what you and I would like to have. . . . David came in and said, "This is how it has to be." . . . He would not negotiate.[16]

As you'll see, Lewis and his colleagues do have their reasons. It's our purpose in this book to help managers see and internalize those reasons, to help them recognize and exploit their own creativity. In many situations, there's a perceived, but unnecessary, rift between managers and creatives. We address this perception with a view to changing it. We want to conceive designers and managers both as makers, in creative partnership to make coherent and resonant special things.

PART TWO

THE COMPONENT
PARTS OF FORM

I

Pattern denotes organization. When you perceive a pattern in nature—the surf booming on the beach, the movement of the stars across the sky—or in a made thing—a painting; a musical composition; or a household product, such as a trash bin or toilet brush—you've detected evidence of some*thing* or some*one* at work behind the scenes: a force of nature or a maker. In this book we'll say little about forces of nature; our interest centers on patterns made by energy that we'll call a maker. A *pattern* stands apart from its background, usually because it *repeats* material from within itself or from elsewhere in a way that suggests deeper purpose or meaning. Often you don't immediately understand the underlying order. You recognize pattern in a flash of intuition that includes a potential for fuller understanding. And it's in your nature as a human being to seek that understanding, to puzzle out the pattern.

2

When we show you this pattern,

you will recognize it as such, and you may reflexively test your intuition by imagining what else might fit with it, where you've seen it before, and what might complete or extend it. Most people will, as well, imagine the completed circle.

3

Consider this sequence of letters: A B A B A B _ _. What letters come next? Most people will say, "A B." If the pattern maker reveals that the next two letters *are* "A B," you probably will decide that you understand the pattern. You "get it." If you encounter another,

A B M C D M _ _

and another

1 4 7 10 _ _

you'll do the same thing again. You probably project "E F" and "13 16" from these two patterns.[1]

If you encounter a design on a fragment of a border from an ancient Greek building that looks like this,

you'll imagine that the next part of the border, the part that's worn away, might have looked like this:

That border can become a famous ancient design called a Greek Key:

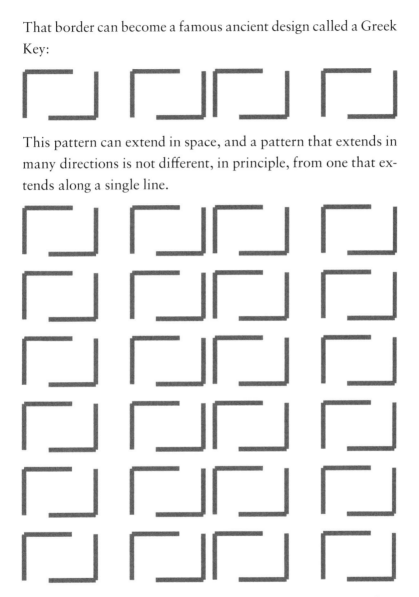

This pattern can extend in space, and a pattern that extends in many directions is not different, in principle, from one that extends along a single line.

These examples show something else: that a pattern often points to something outside itself, a rule or idea that you can use to project the pattern farther. This rule or idea is associated with the pattern. People can (and often do) name such patterns and position them with respect to other patterns to make bigger patterns. Patterns are the building blocks of form. We say a thing exhibits plot when a maker arranges these building blocks into a special thing, such as a carpet.

4

The faculty that psychologists call "pattern recognition" is hard-wired into the human brain.[2] Some biologists see it as a natural feature of brain chemistry, deeply implicated in the evolutionary differentiation of *homo sapiens* from the rest of the animal world.

Sometimes this ability misleads us. So powerful and reflexive is our propensity toward pattern that we sometimes suppose order where none exists. During intense periods of bombing in London during the Second World War, Londoners "devoted considerable effort to interpreting the pattern of German bombing, developing elaborate theories about where the Germans were aiming (and where spies might be hiding because they had been told the pattern)."[3] Years later, William Feller studied the bomb hits and found them to be random, not evidence that the Germans had targeted some areas and not others.[4]

Scientists have words for the tendency to see order when it's not there: *apophenia*, "unmotivated seeing of connections [accompanied by] a specific feeling of abnormal meaningfulness,"[5] and *pareidolia*, the tendency to see something distinct and recognizable in vague imagery or sound (to see the man in the moon, to hear a telephone ring amid the white noise of your shower). People "see" patterns in the stock market (cycles, oscillators),[6] sports (hot shooters, a hitting streak),[7] gambling (a run of black on the roulette wheel),[8] disease incidence ("cancer clusters"),[9] and many other apparently patterned phenomena. People act on their belief that such patterns exist: they buy and sell stocks, change the lineup, bet on red because "it's due," demand action from health authorities.

This ability has also been extremely important to human evolution. Consider this scenario:

You're a hunter almost home at the end of a long day on the savannah, a week's meat for your family slung over one shoulder. Just ahead, behind those bushes, among dark shapes that multiply and shift in the breeze, you see some lines and patches of shadow that add up to something quite a bit like a leopard's spots. It *might* be your imagination. But there's another path just behind you. What should you do?

Take the other path. If you're wrong, if there's no leopard there, it doesn't hurt to act as if there is one. If there *is* a leopard there, though, you took wise steps to protect yourself. In situations like this, to see pattern in randomness is a survival tactic. It puts you a step ahead of the leopard and one up on other hominids who don't have this ability.[10]

This is but one benefit human beings derive from the capacity to discern and conceive pattern. Pattern recognition permits us to use symbols and enables intellectual abstraction. It makes possible language,[11] philosophy, mathematics, art, and—most important for this book—non-ordinary products.

5

The tendency to project extensions and imagine other parts that fit with a pattern arises from a human inclination to make imitations. Delight in imitation issues from both making and appreciating. Think of a baby and mother playing with sound, imitating each other back and forth. This game, universal between mothers and babies, provides an occasion of learning for the baby as he watches Mom's delight in the exchange. The game delights the baby in turn as he becomes better at imitating (repeating) what Mom does and predicting (on the basis of emerging patterns) what she might do next. From his delight he can construct rules for making repetitive patterns that produce the desired affect in his partner. Making and using these rules provides further learning and thus further delight. The baby has a highly evolved instinct to be agreeable; his big head, full of brain, required that he quit the womb early in his development. Unlike most animals, he was born quite helpless and needs a lot of assistance if he's to survive. The baby's big brain, the naturally learned ability to use symbols, and a built-in impulse to create and appreciate imitations—these are part of the same whole.[12] No doubt Aristotle had seen babies and mothers teaching each other when he proposed that "all men delight in imitations. . . . The cause of this is that learning is most pleasant. . . . "[13]

From the elementary rules of this game a child builds up an appreciation of and skill in using the patterns of noise that become language. Children *invent* language as they experiment with these patterns. Our friend's daughter added the contraction "am't" to her English, short for "am not." "Are you going to help your brother?" "No, I am't." Children routinely extend their inventiveness to grammar and syntax as they infer, conceive, and use rules of language. The inclination to complete a pattern thus leads to the development of much more sophisticated abilities.

6

Susanne Langer proposes that a person first apprehends a nonordinary thing (a painting, a nifty gadget) with an intuition. This intuition isn't a process; it's an event. It happens all at once, and cannot be reduced to language. Call it the "Oh, wow!" moment—a "hunch" or a "feeling." It motivates the second stage that Langer calls "contemplation."[14]

Having recognized a thing initially, the observer begins piecemeal to seek its structure, to "reason out" its parts and how the maker arranged them. This *is* a process. It moves step by step, in a dance between intuition and intellect. Each step in reasoning out, or learning, a pattern's structure inspires a new intuition of the emerging whole. And each new intuition drives the observer to further contemplation, further delighted learning.[15]

Simple patterns, such as "A B A B," generalize to a rule. Plot for "A B A B" can be stated as, "Alternate the first two letters of the alphabet," or, more simply, "Repeat the pair 'A B'." This second, simpler version doesn't require knowledge of an additional thing called "the alphabet." But notice—and this is important—the rule that organizes the pattern reaches beyond the pattern; in this beyondness lurk the beginnings of ever more complex structures, of potentially resonant special things.

Having by contemplation conceived a rule for the pattern, having observed the rule's reach beyond the pattern, our observer can use the rule as a guide to further creative activity. A maker builds with an underlying rule that organizes the patterns but can be considered separately from them. Employees at Vipp call this "the company DNA"; they consider it a vital part of the products themselves. It's what's "in there" that makes the products special.

7

Many patterns refer to concepts and things beyond themselves only by convention. We puzzle out the rule within the series "A B A B," but the significance of the arrangement in the word *GANDHI* depends entirely on convention. Our apprehension of a relationship between this word and a particular historical person depends on knowledge that we bring with us, information not contained in the pattern or its rule.

8

Things we observe can be compatible with many different patterns. The series "A B A B __" seems to point to the rule "Repeat the pair 'A B'," but patterns compatible with this series are much more numerous. When we see a few more letters in the pattern, "A B A B C A B C D __," we will likely change our minds about that "repeat the pair" pattern. We can be mistaken about the patterns we think we see, in ways that lead us to revise our understanding when we see more. The fact that multiple patterns can fit with what we observe will be very important, because it leads to the possibility of surprise, when a pattern turns out to be different from what we assumed.

9

Human beings have robust pattern recognition skills. We can distinguish pattern from background even when the pattern's not quite the same each time we see it—say, if it has fuzzy edges, or if part of it's missing. This is a very sophisticated capability. Machines can't do it as well as people can. Patterns with spurious variations, or blurry edges, remain patterns, remain recognizable as such, and remain evocative of shared references that go along with those patterns.[16]

10

The Greeks celebrated the human faculty of pattern recognition by creating a myth in which Mnemosyne (goddess of memory) gave birth to the Muses, one for each of the arts. In *Prometheus Bound*, a tragedy usually attributed to Aeschylus, Prometheus explains his relationship to mankind. Among other things, he says, "I gave to them the mother of all arts, / hard working memory."[17] Since Aeschylus wrote, neuropsychologists have shown us that memory and imagination occupy the same areas of the brain, and that the two faculties work interchangeably.[18]

Memory and imagination function together. People remember the repeated elements in a series or space and they imagine (conceive) the rule that governs their arrangement. Memory *and* imagination must work together to maintain the knowledge and attitudes shared with the maker of a pattern and its rules. In *The Sixth Sense*, Shyamalan drew on his sense of the cultural and artistic experience he shares with his audience when he made a sequence in which (1) a woman shown in closeup in her basement stiffens in surprise, followed by (2) a long shot of her as seen from beside the wine rack. He expected his audience to apprehend the pattern and infer an association from it: "There's someone with her in the basement." This inference, in turn, becomes material from which a large assembly of similar patterns develops into the emerging form that becomes the entire movie.

Without imagination and its hard-working partner, memory, none of this can succeed. Patterns that too greatly tax the memory may escape notice. A pattern that repeats the first twenty-two letters of the alphabet presents greater perceptual and conceptual difficulty than one that repeats the first two letters of the alphabet. It's harder to remember so many letters, so this is a harder pattern to discern.

11

An example that came up in a graduate statistics seminar we took once upon a time asks what a conscientious statistician ought to do if a graph of the data she captures from a natural phenomenon traces out a pattern that looks like this:

This representation of data poses difficulties for a statistician for only one reason: the pattern in a graph of these data looks like a face. The pattern stands out from other data plots because of its similarity to something that the statistician has seen before, a recognizable pattern. This leads to suspicions that the data might be fake. In that seminar, it also led to other fascinating issues, such as, What if it's a face but with one eye in the wrong place? How different from a face must it be to be okay—not to arouse the suspicions of a conscientious statistician?

Though we call references like this face "shared," it's unlikely that everyone experiences the same associations with a given pattern. Some people may see patterns that others don't. Patterns don't convey concepts or ideas from one mind to the next as you might pour a liquid from one glass to another. The concept or idea that ends up in your glass as a result of an encounter with a pattern will differ from the concept or idea that ends up in your friend's glass, even when you encounter the pattern together. Nevertheless, in social settings, as people learn about and relate to others, they effectively negotiate agreements that lead them to share associations. Without these agreements, no one could communicate. To say this in a way currently *en vogue*: shared references are "socially constructed."[19]

It will suffice for our present purposes to assume that people can and do share references; that some references are more obscure (shared by fewer people) than others; and that some are so obscure they may not be shared at all at first, though sharing can be arrived at through contemplation and assisted learning. In some contexts, we may call this kind of assistance "marketing."

12

Trajectory is a path taken by an object moving through space. When an object moves through space (from here to there) it also moves through time (from now 'til then). Trajectory can serve as a metaphor to indicate a path our contemplation takes through the events in a process, across the surface of an object, or among the elements of an idea. *Trajectory* indicates not only where the path has been—in space (over there) or time (back then)—but also how it might continue—through space (around the corner) or time (into the future).

13

The word *trajectory* suggests *direction*, but not necessarily a single direction. A pattern (2, 4, . . .) may suggest more than one rule (counting by 2s, 2, 4, 6 . . .; doubling, 2, 4, 8 . . .; squaring, 2, 4, 16 . . .). A similar principle applies to trajectories. When patterns are placed together, juxtaposed, they can suggest different possible trajectories.

The first few moments of *The Sixth Sense* contain, among many others, the following two patterns. Pattern 1: Anna stiffens in surprise in a long shot of her from beside the wine rack. We've already noted that pattern: "Someone in the house!" Pattern 2: Malcolm and Anna elaborately celebrate his important award for helping troubled mental patients. "Hubris! Possible downfall." In combination, these patterns foreshadow a number of possible trajectories. The movie shows only one of these: Dr. Crowe receives a visit from a mental patient that he did not help as much as he thought he had. This trajectory, in turn, opens up potential for new trajectories, even as it shuts down many others.

Shyamalan put patterns together to suggest these trajectories. Of course as a maker he can't control how individuals will apprehend his patterns and their arrangements; it's not impossible that some spectators will create their own, different trajectories. Everyone, though, will *anticipate* some kind of continuation as a natural consequence of apprehending trajectory. Some may not apprehend or anticipate in the way just described, but Shyamalan has a robust skill at plotting, and if later they think back about

early story events, patterns already encountered, they may realize that those patterns pointed in a now obvious direction, even
if they didn't see it at first.

14
Two points in space

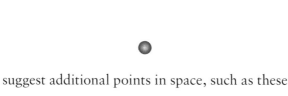

suggest additional points in space, such as these

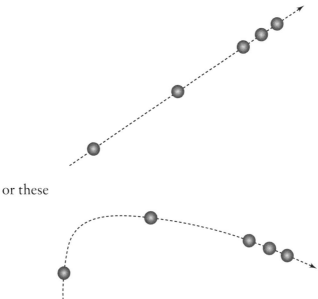

or these

Look what happens when we add a third point. When you engaged with the first two points, your pattern recognition instinct
inclined you to anticipate one or more possible extensions. The
added third point revises and refines those extensions, opening
some doors, closing others.

   The makers of forms that unfold primarily in time, such as
movies, plays, and business services, do something very like this

arranging of points in space as they plot patterns and repeat them. The disturbed visitor who drops in on Crowe and Anna repeats Crowe's diagnosis of him. "Possible mood disorder." A few minutes later in the film (some months later in the story) Crowe begins to work with a new patient, a little boy. The director displays closeups of Crowe's notes, with "Possible mood disorder" circled for emphasis. These two points in the movie (a pattern created in the movie, not brought in by a spectator) create a trajectory with links of similarity (a kind of repetition) to the trajectory that ended with a disturbed young man in Crowe's bathroom. Connect these dots and the trajectory anticipates a future in Crowe's treatment of the new patient that gives him a chance to make up for his past failure. But this trajectory also creates potential for a second failure. And, of course, the consequences of these antecedents might turn out to be even more complicated. (They do.)

15

Trajectory, a movement in both space and time, can also apply usefully to objects. Intuition of a non-ordinary object takes no time: "Oh, wow!" Subsequent contemplation approaches the object piece by piece, an exercise that does take time. As it unfolds before you in time, contemplating a special thing becomes like following the events of a story. Visual feature "follows" visual feature as you make your way through the "events" presented by the object. You may feel as if you have greater control of the sequence of these events, the path your attention traces through them, when contemplating an object in space rather than one that unfolds in time; this is true, but it's a difference in degree, not kind. The maker of a play or movie cannot control the attention of the audience either; he or she depends on the engagement and cooperative inclinations of the audience, its tendency to follow trajectories. We can (and do) cooperate similarly when we engage with objects in space.

16

The Bang & Olufsen Beovision MX series of television sets, designed by David Lewis, had a product lifespan of eighteen years (1986 through 2003) in an industry in which models often live only a few months. One reason for its longevity: Lewis arranged the geometry of the TV to engage, fool, intrigue, and satisfy people's natural interest.

Other CRT TVs had long straight sides stretching back from the front surfaces, creating a deep box full of empty space to accommodate the required distance between a ray source and a screen. But the lines of the MX chassis featured a sharp turn inward a few inches back of the screen surface. From the front and side (the usual viewpoints) the sharp turn created an invitation: "Look this way, please, at this unusual juxtaposition of patterns. What do you think they're up to?"

They're up to something simple, though it took a genius to design it. Placed together in this way, the patterns form a trajectory that in turn creates potential for a flat surface not far behind and parallel to the screen. The set thus appears very flat, decades before today's flat-screen TVs appeared. But how can that be?

Of course the MX needed room for its CRT, so eventually the chassis does turn rearward and extend to the necessary depth. But the trajectory created by patterns on the front and along the side anticipate a flat back for the set (Figure 2.1). You may now imagine a variety of flat backs, and a surface that might turn out to be even more complicated than expected. (It does.) And so on.

As you contemplate this TV, each element of the design (each "event" plotted in the story) will prompt questions about what comes next. And those questions (1) prompt your imagination to create answers and (2) anticipate the next trajectory. In this way, an object invites contemplation as if it was a story and an

FIGURE 2.1. Bang & Olufsen's Beovision MX.
Source: Bang & Olufsen, reprinted by permission.

idea all at once. There's pattern, or trajectory, which leads to
expectations, which are met sometimes. When they're not met,
what happens or appears can seem better than what you might
have expected. This works in time or in space, and in both.

17

Beginning, middle, and end:[20] Earlier we mentioned some patterns—the camera shot next to the wine rack that says, "Someone
in the house!" or recognizable shape elements, such as straight
line, right angle, inward curve—that have no antecedents in the
thing they're building. They're the starting points for trajectories
that might emerge. Nothing within the made thing suggests, de-
fines, or explains them. We intuit and contemplate such patterns
either by decoding an inherent order (for example, repetition in
A B, A B, . . .) or by drawing on our own history and experience.

Henri Poincaré suggests that we perceive space by using our sense of our own bodies as a kinesthetic template. That personal sense of our own body in space becomes the basic unit we use to construct the world around us, measure it, and fix our position within it.[21] Embarking on our experience of a business product or service we locate ourselves with respect to it by using our own histories. A B&O TV doesn't have to introduce us to rectangles, right angles, flat surfaces, and swoopy curves; we know them already, as we already know conventional TVs, and we bring what we know to an event of sympathetic intuition.

But trajectories *do* have antecedents in the made thing. Repetition of "Possible mood disorder" suggests a trajectory for Crowe's relationship with his new patient. Geometric patterns in combination suggest a flat back on the B&O TV. Some patterns and materials have antecedents and consequences in the made thing and some do not. This allows you, when you confront it, to partition a thing into three parts that you can use when you think about the structure of special things: borrowing again from Aristotle, we'll call them beginning, middle, and end. They are the first way to look at the plot of relationships among patterns and trajectories, and at the repetitions that, eventually, create a non-ordinary product's resonant form.

A beginning has nothing before it, and something after. An ending has nothing after it and something before. A middle has both a before and an after. That's a crude paraphrase of Aristotle's definition. Patterns that have no antecedents within the made thing are its *beginning*. A special thing will strike observers at first (intuition) by its arrangements of elements that they mostly bring to the observation. We've all seen many a TV. The Beovision MX will use experience as a starting point for contemplation. *The Sixth Sense* draws heavily on viewer experience of watching thrillers.

Trajectories have antecedents within the beginning; they make up a made thing's *middle*; most made things have middles packed full of trajectories and potential trajectories, possibilities that may or may not become part of the made thing. A thing's middle repeats patterns and materials from the beginning to create its trajectories. The story of *The Sixth Sense* very quickly leaves behind our experience of thrillers and develops our experience of *this* thriller. Most of us never bother to look at the back of a TV, so some elements of its form, many trajectories, may remain hypothetical (which is why David Lewis's flat TV illusion works so well). Let's look at it again. We anticipate a well-made middle on the basis of a thing's beginning; once in the midst, we confirm some of our anticipations, dismiss others, and discover new ones. And finally we recognize the end when a thing presents nothing new to anticipate: no further potential.

Trajectory thus names a relationship among patterns as they precede and follow one another, except for the first, which precedes everything (has consequences—similarities to antecedents) and follows nothing (has no antecedents—nothing similar in the past), and the last, which follows everything (*is* consequences) and precedes nothing (is not antecedent). Again, appreciation of this way that parts of a thing are plotted directs the process of contemplation as a person reasons out a form.

18

Antecedent and consequence refer to time and space, both. The rectangles, right angles, and swoopy curves of the B&O TV open some potentials for the rest of the shape, and shut down others. If you take a look at the back and see how David Lewis resolved those potentials, your pattern recognition instincts will recognize the necessary consequences of the combined rectangles, right angles, curves, and CRT geometry—their plotted similarities.

Let's define *forward* as the relationship of control a pattern (or combination of patterns) exerts over possible extensions (consequences). This control exhibits as similarity, a form of repetition. And let's define *back* as the relationship of similarity between the focus of our attention and its antecedents. Some spatial elements of a thing cut off the possibility of some others; some create a potential for still others.

19

In his play *Of Mice and Men*, John Steinbeck tells a story of two itinerant field hands in the Salinas Valley of California. George looks after and protects Lennie, a simple man incapable of life on his own. The story moves inexorably to a tragic end: Lennie, horribly strong in body and equally weak in mind, inadvertently kills a woman; George, to save Lennie from the lynch mob he can hear approaching, shoots his friend as the curtain falls. In the first scene of the play, George refuses to let Lennie keep a mouse he's caught and accidentally killed while petting it. Here's how this moment appears in the script:

GEORGE (*sternly*): Give it here! (Lennie *reluctantly gives him the mouse.*) What do you want of a dead mouse, anyway?

LENNIE (*in a propositional tone*): I was petting it with my thumb while we walked along.

GEORGE: Well, you ain't pettin' no mice while you walk with me.[22]

The first appearances of these materials (fragile, small creatures, petting soft textures, and so on) establish a trajectory; within the conventions of playmaking, they create a structural anticipation that they will appear again. A playgoer expects materials similar to those of the beginning to appear in the middle and end. This is not an ordinary or "real life" likelihood, it's a technique for making plays. But the materials chosen for repetition here are "like the reality"; that is, they conform to our expectations of everyday life. It's here that confusion can begin; an audience can start expecting the emerging future on the basis of personal experience, rather than on histrionic experience of the play's plot.

Now, when in the first scene of Act III Lennie meets his boss Curley's tiny, very attractive wife in the hayloft, Steinbeck constructs their flirtation out of patterns that first appeared in the scene with the mouse:

LENNIE (*moves close to her*): I like to pet nice things. Once at a fair I
seen some of them long-hair rabbits. And they was nice, you bet.
(*Despairingly.*) I'd even pet mice, but not when I could get nothin
[*sic*] better.[23]

Curley's wife misunderstands Lennie's attraction to her; she thinks it's sexual, when in fact he simply likes to pet nice things. To him she's nice, but when he pets her too hard, she panics. Her struggle panics him. The inevitability of the accidental murder results from Steinbeck's poetic skill, which he has used to establish a trajectory, a potential. When patterns reappear, they connect to their antecedents. This trajectory binds together what spectators may think of as the life-like content (incidents, words, images, and other parts of the play). For Steinbeck, these all were formal elements of a complex design that includes many soft things.[24] You'll find these arrangements of repetition (beginning, middle, end; anticipation, realization) in any carefully made thing.

20

This rearrangement of trajectories gets us to the idea of *closure*.

The simplest form of closure happens when expectations of how a trajectory will continue are confirmed, as the next scene in the movie, say, or as the next feature of a physical object moves around a corner.

A complex closure happens when realization of the next part of a continuing trajectory generates a surprise that changes the possible interpretations of the trajectory's antecedents. Patterns and trajectories shift their meanings and paths, *as you look back.* The pattern you thought was "counting by 2s" turns out to be "squaring." Other patterns may also shift. In a complex object this might have a ripple effect, and you might realize that the trajectories you thought you'd recognized are not the ones you now recognize.

The Sixth Sense contains a dramatic illustration of this. With about ten minutes to go in the movie, Shyamalan presents a pattern that will cause a spectator to reconceive everything seen up to that moment. The situation of the main character turns out to be very, very different from what it seemed to be, and it all goes back to that night of celebration, to that half-naked young man in the bathroom. What apparently was going on isn't at all what was going on.

In *Of Mice and Men*, Lennie's protector becomes his executioner. On the Beovision MX, a flat-backed TV has depth after all.

As you contemplate a special thing, your mind engages the interplay of antecedents and consequences in a process not unlike the dance of intuition and contemplation. The maker provides structural opportunities for you to recognize particular trajectories that relate back to similar patterns—antecedents. From some patterns you imagine trajectories that have different possible consequences. Particular trajectories and their consequences will ultimately appear as the necessary issue of their antecedents because when you retrace the earlier patterns, you'll see the inevitability that derives from repetition, from the relationships of similarity among antecedent and consequential trajectories and their patterns. And although the necessity of this or that pattern could not be seen in prospect, in retrospect, after sufficient contemplation, antecedents become clear and you recognize consequences as inevitable, necessary.

21

Patterns, juxtaposed, combine to suggest trajectories. Trajectories, plotted in various ways, create expectations. Arranged in a beginning, middle, and end, expectations are sometimes met and sometimes not, in closure. These parts together create form (Figure 2.2). These are the component parts of plot, the anatomy of the soul (of design). They exist in time or in space, or in both.

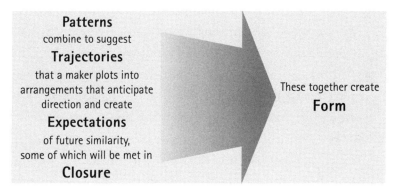

FIGURE 2.2. The Creation of Form Revisited.

22

Remember this song?

1 Three blind mice,

2 Three blind mice.

3 See how they run,

4 See how they run.

5 They all ran after the farmer's wife,

6 Who cut off their tails with a carving knife.

7 Did you ever see such a sight in your life, as

8 Three blind mice?

What patterns do you see and hear within it? What rules and what associations do you conceive from them?[25]

Listen to the song as you sing it aloud. The eight lines contain two repeating melodies, musical patterns. The first, in lines 1, 2, 3, 4, and 8, moves simply down the scale. Three blind mice. It's the same scale for lines 1, 2, and 8; for 3 and 4 the melody starts one note higher. The song uses a more complex melody for lines 5, 6, and 7. These lines repeat exactly, except for a pitch difference that makes the last note of line 7 a bridge to line 8.

The two melodies have different rhythmic patterns. These correspond to the two metrical patterns made by the words. Say the song aloud without singing it. Note the repetitions, and the slight variations caused by particular words needed for the story. The song's plot has verbal patterns within these repetitions. It has eight lines, but only five different ones. Lines end in the same word (mice and run—repetition) or in rhymes (wife, knife, life—aural similarity).

You intuit the patterns in the song as a non-ordinary thing. Then it presents itself to your contemplation. From the patterns emerge trajectories plotted into a form. In this simple example you can see how the patterns together create a whole that escapes description in discursive language. When sung, the ending that repeats the beginning in words and tune "feels" "right." It has the resonance common to special things. That's about all we can say without getting more musically technical, so we'll leave it alone.

Feeling is the kind of word people mostly use to report on their intuitions of form. See a trash bin on display in the Louvre and it grabs you well before you take a seat on the bench and start really looking at it. Other unique forms, even a trash bin, may differ extremely from "Three Blind Mice," but in principle our contemplation of patterns that create trajectories, and then a form with mysterious appeal, will be similar on any occasion, no matter how complex or extensive the special thing.

Taking a simple song apart in contemplation doesn't give us language to explain "feeling." We can't say exactly why the song has strong enough appeal to survive long past its original, socially constructed associations. But obviously there's something important here, something innovators and marketers might want to study. Just think! To make a product for sale that uncountable numbers of widely various people in utterly different situations will use for hundreds of years. As we've said before, it won't be desirable, or even possible, to derive simple formulas to do this, but our reflections on the arrangements that make this simple song non-ordinary will help us make an idea of plot and form, and provide some insight, even some useful generalizations, about this or any other special thing. It may also, when imaginatively combined with your particular knowledge and experience, shed some light on how people who make such products are able do it, or what you might do to help your team.

23

We've said little here about what makes a form "special" or non-ordinary. But clearly a structure that leads to expectations and resolutions can be arranged in a more or less expert way. A product can exhibit expertise in this strict technical sense of having a well-integrated beginning, middle, and end, and of having its patterns connected with each other in trajectories that have connections of similarity to material both forward and back. We propose such technical notions so that we can conceive an idea of pattern, trajectory, and form without falling into a discussion of content, opinions, or taste.

Up to this point, we've also avoided discussing predicted audience (customer) response. As much as it may seem otherwise when you encounter a non-ordinary product that affects you powerfully, your feelings are not a part of that thing. The misapprehension that they are leads to confusion and to unhelpful explanations of why some things sell better than others when they don't work any better.

We're engaging in a rather technical discussion here about pattern, trajectory, and form to show how the features of a made thing relate to one another *independent* of any opinions about the subject, content, or affect that you or individual unknown people (potential customers, say) may have. When notions of content, taste, and affect wander into a discussion of form, assertions get cloudy and unhelpfully sentimental. The structure is the product; responses to it are not. Recognizable content and typical responses to it can obscure perception of a made thing's arrangements of repetition, its formal structure.

So we clearly need a concept that applies to a form and allows us to describe technically the expertness with which its parts are arranged. For this purpose we'll propose an idea we'll call *coherence*, an internal quality of a made thing, and note that coherence can result in *resonance*, the harmonic interaction among parts that has the effect of magnifying the significance of those parts, of increasing their size beyond what could be predicted by taking their sum. These are the subject of Part 3, to which we now turn.

PART THREE

QUALITIES OF THE SOUL (OF DESIGN) AND THEIR CONSEQUENCES

I

Once we saw a production of *Hamlet* in which the director introduced Arab-looking terrorists, complete with robes and AK-47s, as an entourage for Fortinbras when he arrived in Denmark to avenge his father's death. Fortinbras himself was dressed as the other characters, not as an Arab. The terrorists shocked us, as the director intended. He intended a reference to the ongoing life of the audience, to events in the world outside the theatre.

But the terrorists had no antecedents in the play; they issued from no pattern, were part of no trajectory, satisfied or frustrated no expectations arrived at through experience of the play. Appendages rather than parts well integrated into the form, they appeared out of nowhere and they led onward to nowhere.

This play *was* plotted. It had a beginning, middle, and end. It created form from patterns, trajectories, expectations, and closure. But there was something wrong with it. It had appendages in addition to its well-integrated parts. It was, in a word, *incoherent*. It was *poorly* plotted and had an inferior design, a defect in its soul. And it was *not*, therefore, special.[1]

In Part 2 we described how patterns, trajectories, and expectations; beginning, middle, and end; and antecedents and consequences lead to closure and together create form. But as the example above shows, these components can combine without being *well* plotted.

Now we shift focus. We turn from identifying the parts to describing a quality of form that we call *coherence*. This quality, which we introduced in Part 1, arises when all those parts integrate well, when they don't have incongruous appendages or call attention to themselves. Coherence describes how well the parts of a thing fit together. It's a technical description of the internal structure of a made thing, of how well its middles flow from beginnings, its ends from middles.

We'll also examine and reflect on how coherence can result in *resonance*. We introduced resonance as a result of coherence. It is both an intrinsic quality, the result of interaction among the plotted parts, and a source of external affect. It's the quality of a special thing that prompts a sudden intuition of its specialness. When people confront a coherent form they often experience the effects of its resonance, its surprising magnitude. When they do, they use feeling words, such as *special, cool, beautiful, powerful*, and so on.

2

Think back a moment to Susanne Langer's proposal of a two-step process of confrontation with something special. It begins when you intuit the thing's unique appeal: "Oh, wow!" It continues with a period of contemplation, during which you gradually reason out the unique form's principle of organization, its plot.

Human beings can hardly avoid this two-step dance. As Aristotle observed, they delight in learning, and will rarely turn down a chance to perform this sequence. They approach form by seeking to understand the principle that governs the arrangement of its parts. We've called that principle "plot."

You may already know (because of that intuitive flash) that the thing you're contemplating doesn't compare with anything else that you might use to recognize it. Or you might, from intuition, be less certain; maybe you sense something deeper, that you need to puzzle out. You therefore seek to discover the parts of the made thing, and to conceive the principles that plot them into the form before you.

We use the word *conceive* advisedly. Nobody can know what the maker had in mind during the making process. In fact, the energy we call "maker" might be a collaboration, each member of the team working with personal intentions that combine to create a product none of them could individually have conceived. Contemplation is as much a matter of imagination and memory as of observation. This learning and invention accounts for much of the pleasure a person takes in the experience.

3

Aristotle suggested a scheme for organizing this kind of contemplation. In his book *Physics*, he wrote that any made thing can fully be described by identifying its four "causes," the reasons it is the way that it is: a material cause (what it's made of), a formal cause (plot), an efficient cause (who or what made it), and a final cause (the reason for making it).[2] We adapt his terms to suit our purposes.

A maker
Performs operations on *materials*,
Plotting them into a *form* they wouldn't naturally assume,
For a final *purpose*.

By "maker" we don't mean to identify an individual fabricator. We mean simply to insist that a made thing does not arise naturally. The materials, demands of form, and final purposes control the energy needed; the energy available in turn controls the other three causes. In our scheme this energy takes three usual forms; we suppose three kinds of makers: managers, who make a workspace; designers, who conceive (make) special things in imagination; and craftsmen, who fabricate the conceived things in physical materials. We take these up in detail in Part 4.

You can usually identify the parts and reason out, learn, or conceive plot in the form you're contemplating. The materials changed and arranged by a maker, the thing's parts, fall into two categories. Some are aggregate ingredients that you can isolate from the thing: the controls, screen, housing, and so on that make up a television. These parts can be removed or altered without changing a thing's essential coherence.

A made thing has less tangible parts, as well. David Lewis conceived the two centimeters wanted by the engineers not as they did, an aggregate ingredient, but as a quality (call it length) interdependent with other parts (call them width and depth). To change one would reduce plot coherence and reduce or even destroy the resonance that made the TV so attractive in the market. To change one quality demanded that he change both the others.

The made things we're interested in have a double final cause. In the first stage of contemplation, considering the thing itself, independent of relationships with any other thing, the purpose of plot is that helpful tautology: the thing is arranged as it is so that it can be what it is.[3] The second purpose points beyond the thing itself to its function in the business world: to create value. We begin with the first of these two purposes, the handy tautology.

4

First, ask, "What are the parts to this thing?"[4] You needn't rank them; they'll have different importance depending on how you look at them. As the original energy of making did, you'll perform operations on them, placing them in sequences, and noting how, as you conceive their arrangement, they repeat themselves within the systems we've noted: patterns create trajectories that in turn create expectations. The materials themselves condition those expectations.

Second, ask, "How do they fit together?"[5] The task of contemplation at this point becomes one of conceiving relationships. That's the soul of any special thing, plot: the quality of coherently interactive relationships among its various repeated materials.

As you conceive these relationships in more and more detail, your conception of the thing's form will become more and more fully organized and the quality we call coherence more and more clear. In the contemplation process, coherence will seem to appear gradually as you become more and more familiar with the thing, its parts, and the ways they fit together. As you contemplate it, for instance, the parts of a thing will seem to reduce in number as you perceive more and more the similarities and interactions they have with each other. These fewer and fewer ingredients more and more meld together; they exhibit similarity as versions or types of each other. As a result, plot (the patterns you conceive, their trajectories, the range and limits of expectations they contain) becomes tighter and tighter, the bonds among the parts increasingly strong and obvious. As you continue this process of contemplation, you'll come to realize that this quality, plot, is the source of your first intuitive reaction to the special thing. The resonance of its parts led to your intuition. You recognized it as special before you understood any details. That recognition then produced a desire in you to conceive (learn) in depth the form of the thing.

5

We use the words *learn* and *conceive* interchangeably in the context of intuiting plot. The work of reasoning out the coherence of a unique product is both interpretive and creative. Take a look at, or remember, an automobile you admire.[6] It appears in space. It displays horizontal lines. You'll observe that these lines repeat and echo each other in ways comparable to, say, the repetitions and echoes of words and sounds in "Three Blind Mice." The maker has arranged these in variations that enhance your sense of their similarity and suggest onward trajectories. You might remember another car in which the patterns of horizontal lines relate to each other with a similar unifying effect.

You'll also notice that these parts, the horizontal lines, cannot be removed from the car and have it still be that car. We're talking about something different from the cap on a bottle or the handle on a briefcase. You can uncap the Coke bottle and still have a Coke bottle. You can drink the Coke, and it's still a Coke bottle. You can't remove those sexy curves and still have a Coke bottle. The curves and any other parts of this coherent object participate in each other. We say they are interdependent in the same way that the four "causes" are interdependent. The parts are arranged, not merely gathered. Plot, the source of coherence, discriminates a discrete thing from an aggregate of parts. A pathway differs from a pile of gravel. Some made things are more coherent than others, but all have coherence to some or other degree.

6

It's not easy to construct a thing that has a coherence that stops you with an intuitive "Oh, wow!" Here's that Beovision MX from Part 2 again (Figure 3.1).

Look down at the back and you'll discover a line that does not parallel but instead *almost* mirrors the curvature of the screen. From that line, the frame that houses the CRT extends with a concave swoop that also invokes the curved screen. But these lines, and the overall depth of the TV, disappear when you look at the set straight on, as when you watch a program (Figure 3.2).

FIGURE 3.1. Bang & Olufsen's Beovision MX.

Source: Bang & Olufsen, reprinted by permission.

FIGURE 3.2. Front View of the Beovision MX.

Source: Bang & Olufsen, reprinted by permission.

Each choice Lewis made to create this physical form is like a twist in a good story. Designer and poet offer us not the most obvious trajectory, but a more interesting one, one that in hindsight, as we contemplate the whole, flows necessarily from its antecedent patterns: George in *Of Mice and Men* dedicates himself to protecting Lennie, and in the end must kill him; the concave swoop of the Beovision calls attention to the depth of the TV, then causes it to disappear. The new trajectory repeats or echoes patterns from other parts of the structure. At the play's end, George and Lennie recite their ritual dream: a place of their own where they aren't hired hands but work for themselves. "And have rabbits!" says Lennie. The last time Lennie talked about rabbits he petted Curly's wife to death. As the curtain falls, instead of George's ritual answer, "And have rabbits," there's a gunshot. In a similar way, the TV's curves and angles relate to and repeat one another so that when the point of view moves, one image disappears and another takes its place.

Well-constructed plot will not require you to react from your own life experiences. Spectators don't need a degree in psychology to know that the death of Curly's wife is "right." The play provides everything they need. Just so with an object like the B&O TV. You need no understanding of arcane design principles, no prior experience of similar objects, to delight in the coherence of Lewis's design and to respond to the harmonic relationships among its parts. The thing itself has provided all that's needed to learn and appreciate it.

7

As you contemplate the inter-relationships among the parts of a made thing, considerations of coherence can lead to considerations of *magnitude*. The sequence we used to organize our concept of unity (beginning, middle, end) will also help you to think about a thing's appropriate size and shape. Any thing, of course, will have size and shape: it will have extension in space (an object), in time (a process), or in imagination (an idea). In contemplation, special things exhibit magnitude in all three of these realms. We've noted that things with extension in space require time to contemplate them, an activity that takes place in imagination.[7] A thing's beginning, your first intuition of it, happens all at once; it's an event, not a process. But as you contemplate the thing (and contemplation *is* a process), you'll naturally, instinctively make connections among materials of the beginning and new materials in the middle; these connections lead to further materials until the end, at which point they lead no further.

The number and complexity of these connections and the resonance of their interactions create a thing's magnitude. Magnitude means size, of course, but as a tool for thinking about special things, we use it to mean *appropriate* size. By leading a maker to think in detail about dimensions in time and space, and their interdependence, this sequence can help to control those dimensions, can help makers, marketers, and end users come to decisions about closure and value. To achieve its proper magnitude, a thing must have appropriate extension in space, time, and imagination. It must be neither too big nor too small. Too big and none of these people can distinguish it from its surroundings; too small and its parts blur together. It must be neither too long nor too short. Too long and they can't remember the beginning when they get to the end and thus can't tell if it's finished. Too short and they won't notice the progress of its sequences. It must also have an appropriate density of detail: too complex and it's confusing, too simple and it's, well, too simple. In addition, resonant forms differ greatly in the magnitude of their various features. In the play *Hamlet*, the character Hamlet has considerably greater magnitude than his ex-friend Rosencranz.[8]

Patterns, repetitions, and variations must exhibit size and shape appropriate to the patterns, repetitions, and variations that surround them. The elements of magnitude must, as must other features of a coherent form, fit together—must be, like Baby Bear's porridge, "Just right."

8

In a coherent thing, every change, however minor, alters the whole. To keep the whole coherent, a form adjusted in one detail must be adjusted in another, and another, and so on, in a ripple effect until a new coherence is achieved. Changing a detail opens the creative process anew, at which point the maker needs to follow the process to an aesthetically coherent conclusion. David Lewis could not agree to add a mere two centimeters to the back of his classic MX TV design. For him there was no "mere" about it. In the event, he made the thing two centimeters longer but also made the ripple effect adjustments required by that change. He reconceived the product into an entirely new design. None of us, looking at the new design, is likely to notice any difference without measuring. That's Lewis's success exactly.

In our research, we've seen this concern again and again. At e-Types, a Danish design firm, a designer told us that he wouldn't change a color for a customer; he'd "rather make a whole new thing." Jonas Hecksher, the e-Types creative director, described how he arrived at a coherent design for labeling on a beer bottle and how he made the beer company executives *physically* aware of that coherence:

We got a lot of beers and drank the beer and thought of colors. This one [holding up a bottle][9] is brandy wheat, and made of apples, so it has a fruity, apple taste. But it's not red apples; it's green apples. . . . So we put the strong citrus of green apple inside the letters on the label. We did that for a lot of colors. Then we went to [company executives] and said

"Now we have to taste the colors of this beer." And they all sat with us and tasted. We put the wrong color up [while they tasted] and then put up the right color, and they could see what was the right color.

A couple of weeks after the tasting, the beer company's marketing department convinced company executives that the colors chosen by the designers were "not strong enough." Hecksher reconvened the executives who'd been involved in the tasting:

They came back and said, "We'd like a little more strong colors." But we said, "You remember, you were sitting tasting? If you want to do the finest beer, you know you have to go for an original taste, the flavor? Well, you don't compromise on beer, so don't compromise on look." . . . It's important. If this [holding up one labeled beer bottle] was on this one [holding up another]—if it was blue, it would be the wrong taste. It's very important that everything is right, so you're telling the same story.[10]

The execs left convinced and the beer launched to great success.

Our visits to Vipp gave us another set of revealing examples. In one instance, we learned that the company once packed its luxurious towels in cylindrical boxes. But when the display designers tested this idea with customers, it didn't succeed. Customers want to be able to feel towels. There's a serious disconnect between the luxurious texture of the towels and the harsh slick surfaces of a cardboard tube. Vipp's designers concluded that the package-towel combination displayed inadequate plot; it lacked coherence. The company abandoned this experiment.

But it took a different route when it came to packaging a soap dispenser. Vipp put the soap dispensers in stark white boxes, with little print and no illustration. The idea: displays assembled from such boxes could be unusual, dramatic, and distinctive. But when the designers tested the boxes alongside those of competitors, most of which bore a brightly colored photograph of the product, the white boxes faded away. "When we saw them in those big department stores," said Sofie Egelund, lead graphic designer for Vipp, "it didn't work."

But this time Vipp decided to *keep* the white boxes. Sofie explained, "We think that when we will have more of those white boxes, when we make our own shops, or shop-in-shop displays, we will have the possibilities of making some walls, making some room [separate from the other companies' boxes], which will be the Vipp room, and then the white boxes will work very well."

The white boxes anchored an emerging, coherent display concept in which the boxes could resonate in arrangement with all the other elements. The answer, then, was not to abandon them, as they did the incoherent rolled-up-towel-in-a-box concept, but to create a new form—to supply the other parts of an emerging, non-ordinary idea. Vipp arranged all the elements of the display: boxes, stacks of boxes, pedestals and shelves, space between boxes, contrast with adjacent displays of other products, signs identifying the Vipp products, prices, and so on. These arrangements had distinct boundaries that isolated the display, called attention to it, and gave it an appropriate magnitude. The display had, in other words, the quality of plot. The different products, each itself carefully plotted, became interdependent parts of a larger unit, coherently plotted and advantageously set apart from the presentations of the competition.

9

At a business school seminar we attended, a renowned marketing professor observed that live-action movies need real actors, who cost a lot and have complicated schedules. Scenes get filmed out of order, often scheduled according to the actor's availability. This allows little or no opportunity to reconsider a scene some time after it's been shot and decide to do it differently. The actor's already gone. But animation is different, he said. Animated characters don't have schedules, and scenes can be redone later, even much later, as needed. The marketing professor then proposed that moviemakers in the animated feature business might film scenes, then take them to focus groups or apply other market research tools to them. By testing each scene this way and adjusting it on the basis of how well it played with an audience, he suggested, a studio could compose a feature out of scenes already proven to be individually terrific. The overall movie, he reasoned, would be more likely to be a hit.

Ed Catmull, president of Pixar and Disney Animation, who was giving the seminar, disagreed. "We've fooled around with that a bit," he said, "and it generates stories that aren't really good enough." That was that, the answer much shorter than the question.

Ten minutes later, the marketing professor, perhaps unable to believe that Catmull had heard his question correctly, tried again. He rephrased and repeated his original question. Catmull answered it again: "That just doesn't work very well," he said. "The pieces might be great, but the overall story doesn't work."

We heard a similar idea expressed at Vipp, as Sofie Egelund spoke about how they designed their soap dispenser:

Some customers told us that we could make a soap dispenser just by scaling down the bin and putting a pump on the top. [She lifts her hands and shakes her head in a gesture of exasperation].[11] But, you know, it would have been terrible just to make a copy-paste of the bin and make it a soap dispenser. . . . They had a need for a soap dispenser, and they liked the other design [the bin], so, "Why don't you make a mix up of those two?" And we sell a lot of bins, so, "Why don't you just make a bin for a soap dispenser?" . . . But if we make a Vipp bin that's a hanger, or soap dispenser, or a toilet brush, everything, then we will not be here in two years. People might be interested in the beginning, but then, no.

As Egelund and Catmull make clear, gluing great parts together does not make a great whole. Parts unremarkable by themselves can come together into an extraordinary whole. But parts, even great parts, won't "add up" into a great whole the way the marketing professor or some of Vipp's customers suggest. They'll remain an aggregation, a pile of gravel, not a path.

These stories illustrate why plot, coherence, and resonance need to be part of the conversation in a creative enterprise. The success of businesses such as Pixar, Vipp, or e-Types depends on their skill in plotting the coherence of the things they make. Observers of such businesses also need to understand plot, coherence, and resonance, to make sense of what they see. Absent such understanding, Vipp's abandoning the towel boxes while creating a stand-alone display concept and keeping the soap dispenser boxes appears inconsistent. For observers who understand coherence, the actions make perfect sense.

10

Plot, coherence, and resonance, as we've said, are qualities of the internal construction of a made thing. They are *not* a response to the thing. Resonance, because it's physical, shows this most clearly. Of course people respond to resonance—remember the example of Robertson's violin—but their response isn't wood, varnish, and shape. But, they *do* respond, so we can't keep avoiding a discussion of the affective potential built into the structures we've described as aloof and self-referential.

A non-ordinary product affects you, but it affects *you*, an individual. Your technical examination of its formal arrangements may suggest potential success in the market, but that won't help you predict the particulars of its impact on individual persons unknown. Nevertheless, the feelings no one can predict reside *as potential* in a form. Call this "affective significance." A self-referential form doesn't contain feelings, but it can be plotted so as to have a potential to elicit them in, say, a customer.

Let's elaborate on this a bit. Writing of a product's self-contained structure, we've used the word *expectation* to label the potential of a trajectory. There's a possibility here for misunderstanding. Ascribing intention to an inanimate object, no matter how unusual that object, opens a door. It might seem as if an observer does this expecting. But that's not what we mean. We want to keep the observer out of it for a while longer. The *structure* anticipates, by its plot, how trajectories might continue to their consequences. This structure consists in relationships among its parts. In the products we're considering, each one of a kind, these relationships are self-referential, intrinsic. But they include affective significance.

Though intrinsic and self-referential, these relationships have the potential to *elicit* feelings among customers, persons who might want to own and use the product (or service). Such affect, strictly speaking unpredictable, is not a part of the product. The product has its completed form; *that form* has affective significance. When we introduce the idea of affective significance, the observer we've imagined, who intuits, then contemplates the made thing, reasoning out its self-referential form, steps aside, in our imagination, to make room for the next observer, a customer.

In other words, as you learn the parts of a thing and the ways they fit together, you'll experience the form, and part of that experience will be feelings, starting with the "Oh, wow!" of intuition, and in the best case ending with "Gotta have one."

We don't predict the content or form of those feelings; only that you'll have them. As the special thing is unique, so is each person who contemplates it, and so are the feelings generated. In addition, the "meaning" of these feelings changes when the person's activity shifts from contemplation of form to considerations of ownership and use.

We used the word *realization* to label plotting that points back to antecedents. Now we add affective significance. How can you use this idea to help you reason out a non-ordinary form?

Looking back to antecedents, you'll experience two kinds of affect. First, you might have been right or wrong in your anticipations, but now, looking back, you can realize the full trajectory, and that knowledge affords you the pleasures of recognition (of similarities) and learning (their plotted arrangements). There's pleasure merely in seeing the trajectory come into view. Lennie has killed Curley's wife accidentally, just as he did the mouse, you can see that now; accidentally, sure, but the "Of course!" feeling of inevitability might take your breath away. Second, you realize that although the consequence is structurally inevitable, the relationship between the antecedent and consequence is not the similarity you had in mind but is unexpected. Lennie didn't deserve his misfortune; in a successful making process, when there's no similarity between antecedents and consequences the happy shock of serendipity creates the affective significance.[12]

I I

The idea, affective significance, helps with the discipline we spoke of earlier; it gives you a way to prevent corruption of the non-ordinary product by including purposes beyond the realization of its unique form. Later, when the non-ordinary product is manufactured and offered for sale, it will take a different position in your consideration. Instead of learning its form, you can begin to think about its potential to create value in a market.

I 2

When you observe an object located primarily in space, or an idea located in imagination, it gets trickier to apply this concept. The pleasure of recognition, as you learn how parts connect in a surprising way, that's straightforward. Again, there's pleasure as you see the geographical coherence come clearly into view. But in a TV set there's no person, like Lennie, who suffers misfortune.

Even so, there *is* a tension between the structural inevitability of what's visible and other possible ways the trajectories might have resolved. When you contemplate these alternatives, the special thing provides further learning pleasure as you reason out both what you see and other implications, the roads not taken. You might have expected several possible resolutions of the lines in a TV's physical design, and when you come to see the one that is realized, when you come to understand its inevitability, you might feel a tinge of regret for possibilities not realized, possibilities just as likely as the realized ones but which didn't fit as well with their surrounding structure. The maker chose patterns or points to complete the trajectory for reasons that had nothing to do with those patterns or points themselves, and everything to do with their interdependence, with each other and with the rest of the emerging form. Those curves on the back of the B&O TV didn't become the design because they're the prettiest curves David Lewis could draw, but because they fit best with the rest of the TV.

13

In Part 2 we introduced the idea of closure. Now we point out a new implication of closure: it can cause you to reconceive the affective significance of an emerging form.

A maker can end a trajectory with a simple closure. Boy meets girl, boy loses girl, boy gets girl. The pitiable misfortune (boy loses girl) turns out okay after all (boy gets girl). Anticipation and realization resolve into an expected satisfaction—emphasis on *expected*. The story begins happily, the characters suffer a bit, and the story ends happily.

Let's look at a complex closure. Henry Becque, in his play *The Woman of Paris*, makes a nice complex closure in an early scene. He presents a couple bickering: the man jealous, the woman teasing him. As this goes on, spectators observe what appear to be the long-established rites and rituals of a marriage: perhaps not entirely harmonious, perhaps even dysfunctional, but patterns recognizable to anyone who has lived in a family and seen a lot of plays. Then:

LAFONT: As long as you are faithful to me, you are good and honorable; the day you deceive me—

CLOTHILDE (*stops him, goes a little way toward the second rear door and then comes back*): Look out; here's my husband![13]

Affective significance here resides in the writer's sudden addition of a new pattern to an established trajectory. He presented what appeared to be a married couple. When Clothilde's husband enters, that changes drastically. Everything leading up to this sudden surprise now has new significance. But surprise quickly morphs into recognition of new relationships among the play's patterns. On the Bang & Olufsen TV, the repeated and echoed lines of the front create a shallow object; step far enough to one side or peek over the top and a new pattern appears.

Suddenly it's not shallow at all; those lines point to something completely different. "Aha!" And a new intuition provides new material for contemplation, new pleasure in reasoning out the form of this special thing.

In a classic tragedy, undeserved misfortune turns out to be deserved after all. This too is surprising. The affective significance of such a structure is not pity, but something else, perhaps a sense that there's a deep order to life. Consider this arrangement of events.

Anticipation   Boy meets girl: Romeo and Juliet meet at a party.

Realization   Boy gets girl: They fall in love, and spend a night together.

Realization   Boy loses girl: Impetuous Romeo kills Juliet's cousin, and the Prince banishes him.

Complex Closure   Boy gets girl: With help, Romeo and Juliet make a plan that will reunite them forever. But the very impetuosity that fueled their passion undoes their plan. Both die. They're together, but in an unexpected way. Their feuding families reconcile.

The final incidents (clandestine meeting in a tomb, a potion, a dagger, a poison) force the spectators to reconceive the events that led up to them: they now realize that the lovers meet their fate because of *who they are*, as a deserved result of actions they take themselves. The affective significance of these trajectories has changed completely. In his play, Shakespeare nails down this closure with a scene in which the feuding families take responsibility for the deaths of their children.[14]

14

Harold Arlen wrote the song "Over the Rainbow," with lyrics by E. Y. Harburg, for the movie *The Wizard of Oz*; Judy Garland sang it in the character of Dorothy, and stole the show. Over the years it became her signature song. Say "somewhere over the rainbow" and almost anyone will hear, in their mind's ear, Garland singing, or at least remembered snatches of the song. Many other singers performed this song, of course, but no one replaced Garland's rendition.

Until Eva Cassidy. Cassidy died from melanoma in 1996, at age thirty-three. In 1992 she recorded a haunting cover of

Garland's song. Except in the collections of a few fans, the recording went unnoticed until 2000, when Terry Wogan played the song on BBC's Radio Two; it generated an overwhelming response from listeners and quickly became the most requested song in the history of the show. Eva Cassidy albums climbed to the top of the charts in many countries and sold millions of copies.

What strikes us most about Eva Cassidy's version, besides our sense of its musical beauty (that is, our individual responses to its affective significance, confirmed as not unusual by those sales figures), is how seldom it follows the melody of the original. Ms. Cassidy sang jazz, and in "Over the Rainbow" she constructed melodies that echo, repeat, vary from, and circle around Arlen's original. She makes of the old song a new, unique thing. She replicates the original melody in bits within her version; the original lives in those fleeting moments. Her singing creates dense networks of antecedents and consequences, of anticipation, realization, and closure both simple and complex. At each moment the song anticipates the Garland melody, which in turn anticipates Cassidy's variation, sometimes obviously, sometimes subtly, sometimes even sneakily. You can observe all this technically; all of it is a matter of the structure of the thing, not of your reaction to it.

But of course each of her interpolations, each of her interrupted or realized trajectories, has affective significance. The significances attend both her invocations (by repeating bits) of the Garland version and her own melodic and rhythmic extrapolations of that version: the two combine to create a new song. The affective significance of this extraordinary song includes suggested, but not actualized, trajectories begun by the fleeting bits of the Garland version that she uses to make her own song. Each Garland bit creates an occasion for intuition; then, beneath the Cassidy song, shadow trajectories make their way to closure.

When we listen to this song we perform a version of the dance between intuition (delighted recognition of the Garland version) and contemplation (construction of memories of the Garland version, comparison of those memories with the ongoing Cassidy cover, and apprehension of Cassidy's song as a musical form containing both her music and our imagined recollection of Garland). It's not hard to recognize in this dance the pleasures of imitation and learning. And we, the authors, bet you'll experience something very similar when you hear the song.

A special form may not overtly realize all the trajectories it suggests. But Cassidy's "Over the Rainbow" shows that the shadows can make an important part of a complex whole. The Cassidy version achieves a simple closure, even as its form becomes ever more complicated. The Cassidy "Over the Rainbow" has its own complete form, but includes as part of that form the shadow trajectories of Garland's performance, antecedents that Cassidy invites a listener to bring to the experience.

An apprehension of this kind of structure is vital to all makers, especially managers of creatives. In Part 4 we'll have more to say about the difficulties inherent in the traditional, Taylorized, top-down relationships among makers in a creative economy. For now, bear in mind that none of the makers will replicate the song you sing. They'll hear instead a song they make, using as materials your song together with the ones in their heads. You cannot traditionally manage, control, or predict those songs, but you must imagine enough of them to conceive a coherent new song (or product or idea) out of the combination of what you know (shadow trajectories) and what you hear (emerging form). As you, the manager, listen in ways that are increasingly removed from similarity to their antecedents in "real life," you will strive to imagine new connections among materials; new relationships of antecedents, consequences, and reconceptions; and new kinds of closure, both simple and complex.

15

Many years ago, farm equipment maker John Deere made a TV commercial that featured two old men in rocking chairs on a porch, obviously looking at something out in the middle distance. One presents the intuition, unconnected to anything else: "That thing sure is beautiful." The camera pans to include what they're looking at. It's a John Deere tractor out there in the sunshine, gleaming in green and yellow perfection. The second man shakes his head and begins an evaluation of the thing's potential to create value: "Beautiful don't cut oats," he says. "Let's see if it works."

In our reflections on non-ordinary products, we've addressed internal construction, focusing on the describable aspects of their formal structure. But now and again, as our reflections have progressed, the concept of a practical purpose—a need to cut oats—has sneaked in. What's the point of the making activities we're describing? Why worry about plot, coherence, and resonance at all, as long as the thing works? As we've seen, there are reasons—business reasons. Non-ordinary products have a way of selling in greater numbers for higher prices than their ordinary competition.

A new product, an original, coherent form, is new to the world and not yet encountered by people in the world, not in that specific form. People have seen a trashcan or a play, but not this one. So it's hard to say, when the new thing first appears, how well it will achieve its second purpose, useful impact on the world. We can't reliably judge this on the basis of comparison with past, different things.

Oh, people try. The movie industry is great at this. But as Arthur De Vany, using his own special brand of rocket science to analyze returns in the industry, has concluded,[15] and as William Goldman colorfully summarized years earlier, when it comes to predicting a successful movie, "Nobody knows anything."[16] Movie history is full of stories like the one about how wise studio execs passed on the project that became *Star Wars* because it had, they said, narrow appeal. Other creative firms that sell special products tell similar tales. Many of the most interesting breakthroughs would not have appeared without clandestine projects or creative staff who disobeyed managers' orders about what to work on. Much to the dismay of many managers and marketing professors, you can't say, "This song will be special because it has a bass line similar to that hit." You might experience short-term commercial success with such copycats, but that's a different business strategy than the one we're looking at; it's not the route to something special.

Non-ordinary products challenge business logics that are based on statistical frequencies of their isolated features, occurrences of colors or shapes, or particular actors or directors or bass lines. The reason, of course, is the resonance of a special thing, which causes an increase in magnitude that transcends the sum of its individual parts. In statistical terms, each new coherent form draws from a new population. Consequently, processes that aim to understand the useful final cause, including the commercial potential, of a new special thing must be, in the words of Charles Sanders Peirce, *abductive*, based on the notion that such things reveal their purpose only through the unfolding of events.[17] Every new thing is new in its own way, and its audience must contemplate its novelty and discover (conceive) the reasons for it. An audience (customer) may need help in the discovery process from a special sort of marketing.

16

People in creative firms work on both purposes, internal coherence and external effect, at the same time, taking care—in smart companies—to pursue each purpose with appropriate discipline and not to let one gain priority over the other. This results in dynamic evolution for an emerging form and many difficult but productive discussions about trade-offs on the way to closure.

Some who have studied such discussions have reached dire conclusions about the prospects of the first, self-referential purpose. Eikhof and Haunschild studied Germany's publicly funded theater companies, which operate under a policy of *kunstfreiheit*, or "freedom of art" from non-aesthetic pressures, and concluded that even in such protected conditions "economic logics tend to crowd out artistic logics and thus endanger the resources vital to creative production."[18] Despite pessimism like this, creative companies do somehow, sometimes, get special things to market.

But the potential for trade-offs, even destructive conflict, between the two purposes is real. At Bang & Olufsen, David Lewis expressed this concern in our interview with him, as he fretted about increasing time-to-market pressures on his design process, pressures generated by the business side of the company:

This is the problem with having a very narrow time limit and having a very wide portfolio: the time that is necessary to think, and to get above all that [worries about competition, need to make fast decisions] is being reduced so much that maybe—maybe—it might start degrading the quality.

By "quality," Lewis refers, of course, to design quality, coherence. Bang & Olufsen, aware of this potential problem, relies on freelance designers. Some, like Lewis, have a long-term relationship with B&O, but the fact that the designers don't actually work for the company, that they're not employees, provides a check against commercial concerns becoming too pressing. Design director Flemming Møller Pedersen explains:

We don't want [designers] to be [unduly] influenced by other parts of the organization . . . [which have] to worry about optimizing the daily business. [Designers] don't need to understand our industrial limitations . . . manufacturability or what sound can come out of which form. Designers have to be free to look in an unconditioned way at what's happening in our society, how people live and furnish their homes, and then come up with proposals that could be good for B&O. It's up to our engineers to make it work.[19]

At the same time, aesthetic concerns mustn't dominate, either. Then-CEO Torben Ballegaard Sørensen pointed to this danger in noting, "Good designers are strong personalities. They are dangerous because they can walk out on a cliff if that's what they think they should do, but they are valuable because of their own strong interpretation of what you and I would like to have."[20] Part of his job, Sørensen told us, is to prevent strong personalities like Lewis from taking the company off the side of a cliff, even when their sensibilities suggest that it might be interesting.

Sørensen's statement contains another implication important for business managers to keep in mind: when designers like Lewis wander out to the cliff, to the consternation of managers, *they're doing what they're paid to do.* To have a shot at the special, that's how they must behave. Other people need to worry about the potential dangers involved. Lewis might seem unreasonable for not allowing the back of his TV to be extended two centimeters, but if members of your creative staff aren't similarly unreasonable, they're not earning their pay. Creative staffs are supposed to take uncompromising positions, however unbusinesslike, even maddening, those positions might seem to a conscientious manager. There are two things to bear in mind here: (1) Lewis *did* fix the problem, and (2) we will shortly present a different way to look at these relationships.

As we've noted though, even in industrial structures, intransigence by creative staff can pay commercial dividends. *Star Wars* made it to theaters. According to Paul Ulrik Skifter, a former Bang & Olufsen CFO, "The only time we did market research was with the Beogram 4000, a record turntable. Marketing people said it would sell fifteen units in Denmark and fifty in the world. It turned out to be one of our most successful products."[21] Sofie Egelund told us the story of how her mother, Jette, created a successful product, helpfully ignorant of conventional business wisdom:

At a time when the company was very small my mother decided to make a toilet brush. . . . She had an idea of how it should look, so she started by making [a prototype]. She didn't start by researching the market, because if she had done that she would have found out that there were ten thousand toilet brushes in the world already, and they were not very expensive. . . . She showed it to some of our good dealers in Copenhagen . . . and the first thing they asked was, "What will the price be?" And she said, "Oh, I think it will be around a thousand Danish kroner" [then about €135 or $150], and they were almost fainting because it was so expensive. They said, "You cannot sell a toilet brush at a thousand Danish kroner." But she believed in this product. Now it sells in the very big department stores. . . . It sells more than this very nice Philippe Starck toilet brush, which costs one-fourth the Vipp brush.[22]

Of course, not every example of creative intransigence results in commercial success. In fact, there's no *necessary* relationship between skillful plotting and commercial success. Sometimes a product is too strange, or appears too early, and not enough can be done about that. A new thing will often appear formless. But sometimes a company can take steps to help a market appreciate a new form.

17

Sometimes we encounter products in which the two purposes seem to converge. The patterns that together create trajectories, the materials that make up a coherent form, can be functional as well as visual. We have distinguished between form and function, but in fact, function determines form and vice versa. The way a thing does something in the world must be part of its structure. Striking examples that combine form and function show us that this is true. Sometimes beautiful does cut oats, and that cutting, the way it unfolds, can exhibit also plot, coherence, and resonance.

Remember, however: beauty and coherence, even resonance, are not synonymous. In its purest manifestations, a relationship between a coherent form and a practical purpose needn't include beauty, or even attractiveness.

Figure 3.3 displays a special thing for which beauty (however defined) isn't a consideration. It's all purpose. But it has plot, and its coherence has a resonance that makes the whole greater than the sum of its parts. The bridge has a single function, to get a load across the creek. It has a grand plot that arranges two subplots, the elements of which interact with each other. The interacting subplots create an aesthetic coherence that resonates to make the whole greater than the sum of its parts. If you're in the business of making special things, or sending them to market, you'll do well to study not-new, homely special things like this bridge. It's a way to sharpen your senses; also, you can practice trusting your intuitive "get it" machinery for the work of making hard choices about closure.

FIGURE 3.3.　A Simple Pratt Bridge.
Source: Image courtesy of J. A. Barker Engineering, Bloomington, Indiana.
Reprinted by permission.

The first plot arranges the bridge's task: the work it must do to get a load across the creek. Its structure also has plot, the arrangement of materials into the object you see. To puzzle out this form you will contemplate these plots one at a time, but they're inextricably combined and can be kept separate only in your imagination in order to contemplate them.

To accomplish its large purpose, the bridge must do two things. It must keep itself from collapsing into the water, and it must prevent distortion of the roadbed so that it doesn't flex and toss the load into the creek. Here's the work plot. The weight of the load creates tension in the girders beneath the roadbed. The bridge responds by distributing that moving tension from wherever it is on the roadbed, delivering it as compression to the piers at either end and as tension to the arch. The X-cross beams along the sides keep the steel members square and plumb, steady under the pulsations of a moving load, maintaining position instead of themselves tipping over into the creek. The first stress hits the roadbed as the load moves past the pier, out over the creek. The roadbed girders want to sag under the load, but the diagonals in each cube take that tension and pass it up to the arch. The diagonals and the verticals pull down on the upper structure, compressing the perpendicular units in the cubes. But that upper structure, an arch, in turn shifts both static and dynamic compression loads toward the prisms at the ends of the bridge, thus transferring them to piers solidly anchored in the ground. In the final bit of work, the prisms push the piers apart, and the girders beneath the roadbed take up that load as tension. Everything is balanced against everything else. Make any changes and everything goes haywire.

Here's the structure plot. You see girders arranged in large units: three cubes (the center) and two rectangular prisms (each end). The prisms connect the piers and the roadbed to the three cubes. The X-cross beams along the sides keep the several units square and plumb. The prisms attach the bridge to the road, and to the piers on which the roadbed rests.

Neither plot has significance absent the other. Neither can function without the other. You can see from our description how impossible they are to separate; to describe one you must invoke the other. And together they create a resonance that makes reasoning out the form, appreciating this homely object, a source of pleasure.

18

Plot arranges everything toward coherence, which leads to resonance, which leads to external effect, such as positive customer affect and commercial value. When a design plays out this way, business is good.

But it doesn't always.

A maker can fail to plot a coherent thing. Customers can fail to perceive the coherence and thus fail to experience its resonance. Then customer affection and commercial value do not follow.

In Part 4, we reconceive the challenges of making and marketing special things in business.

PART FOUR

MAKERS AND CREATIVITY
Toward Commercial Success with Special Things

I

Finnegans Wake by James Joyce, considered by many one of the greatest literary works ever composed in English, might at the same time be one of the least accessible novels ever written in English. Here's the first sentence:

riverrun, past Eve and Adam's, from swerve of shore to bend of bay, brings us by a commodius vicus of recirculation back to Howth Castle and Environs.[1]

To begin to see patterns within even this first line we need, at the very least, to have some knowledge of Irish history (Howth Castle), Dublin geography (riverrun, Eve and Adam's [a pub near Eve's quay on the River Liffey], swerve of shore to bend of bay), and the philosophical and historical works of Giambattista Vico, 1668–1744 (commodius vicus).

You might realize that this first line is the end of a sentence, and you'd find out later (if you made it all the way through) that the book's ending is also a fragment, the beginning of a sentence: "A way a lone a last a loved a long the"—. It's the beginning of that first sentence, in fact: "A way a lone a last a loved a long the riverrun, past Eve and Adam's, from swerve of shore to bend of bay, brings us by a commodius vicus of recirculation back to Howth Castle and Environs."

Finnegans Wake ends where it began and begins at its own ending. You might then, if you know something about Vico, realize that this cyclical structure aligns with Vico's cyclical view of history. If we go no further with this analysis (we won't), you can reasonably infer that this isn't the only way Joyce wove together the materials of this book; you can presume that *Finnegans Wake* has a formal plot structure.

Published in 1939, the book is still in print. Given its longevity, its meaningfulness to people over a long period of time, perhaps we can agree to call *Finnegans Wake* a special thing. It has an internal coherence; it's bigger than the sum of its parts. Even though we, as non-expert readers, can't necessarily see, or fully see, the coherence in the book, perhaps we can accept the views of people who have dedicated time to the book that it is well-plotted and non-ordinary.

The example of *Finnegans Wake*, even though it is a work of art, will help us see that to achieve commercial success, a business-made special thing must meet two challenging requirements. First, a coherent plot must somehow come into existence; in a business, to get this to happen, management must create conditions in which creative workers can thrive, often doing work the manager doesn't understand. Second, management and marketing must help potential customers contemplate and reason out the form, thus to experience the coherence, resonance, and resulting affect that constitutes the special experience of the thing. Like *Finnegans Wake* to the average reader, a special thing it may well be but the average person who encounters it can't properly apprehend it. And a special thing with coherence invisible to most will not succeed commercially.

When first published, *Finnegans Wake* baffled (even angered) most readers. That has changed. Few would now dispute its coherence. Though it didn't arise in a business setting, Joyce himself met the first challenge: he brought a coherent thing into existence.

And yet few can vouch for its coherence directly, because it's inaccessible. Its success with the second challenge then is modest, though probably greater than you might realize. It's in print seventy-plus years after its first publication. For the five years ending in February 2006 (the latest figures we could find), nearly forty thousand copies *"at the very least"* were sold in the United States (a number big enough to hold the attention of most business book publishers).[2] This ongoing success depends in large part on an unlikely consortium of marketers: professors at colleges and universities. College professors include the book in course after course, and every year a new crop of young people learns to apprehend and appreciate its form.

Marketing for special things, then, has to do with preparing customers better to see patterns, trajectory, consequences, and their forms. In some businesses, this might entail some kind of "education" for customers, though perhaps not formal instruction. At the design firm IDEO, CEO David Kelley jokes about a first client meeting, saying, "We haven't trained them yet" to explain that that's why they're meeting in a conference room rather than in the design studio.[3] We described earlier how the chief designer of e-Types orchestrated a beer tasting for client executives to help them understand the logic behind the color choices in his proposed design. In that meeting, he brought the executives back to the moment of intuition, that event in which they "got it," and went on to help them reason out again what they'd gotten. In other words, marketing might borrow from the thing marketed and introduce potential customers to the pleasures of learning, of reasoning out the form.

The commercial challenge associated with special things then is pretty simple. It has these two parts: (1) to nurture special things into existence and (2) to provide information, education, and other assistance to the audience or customers that allows them to perceive a special thing's coherence. As *Finnegans Wake* makes clear, the two challenges interact. The patterns in the book are so exotic that most people will need some kind of help to see them. Marketers have an understandable preference for patterns and forms more accessible than these; they may try to influence the creation of a special thing, perhaps without sufficient regard to the intrinsic qualities of the form. There's a tension to manage here.

2

Artists sometimes assert that they care nothing for accessibility, or for the effects their work might have on the external world. More than once we heard this, or its equivalent, in an interview: "I didn't care anything about 'who's this for,' I'm doing it for me." For makers, turning away from external influences can be part of the way they avoid distractions that interfere with their efforts to create coherence.

But a business must care about who it's for. Managers, quite appropriately, care whether the effects of a made thing will convince customers to buy it. If you're a marketer, tasked with promotion and distribution, you'll have an interest in whether and how you can increase such effects. Can you convince customers to want your special thing? Can you convince more customers? To want it more and to want more of it?

Disagreements between makers and marketers arise from this difference in their inclinations. Marketers have inclinations that make them want to do more of what has worked in the past. That seems a safer way to achieve commercial success. But makers of special things naturally resist this idea. For them, a special thing needs to be new and coherent, and coherence is an intrinsic matter. Usually, makers don't want to play it safe.

3

Not infrequently, creating a special thing depends on overcoming the conventional inclinations of marketers. In the late 1990s teams at Activision instituted a "staged" process to manage uncertainty in the video games business. They designed their "Greenlight Process"[4] to "weed out the less successful games earlier in the [development] process," before too much money had been spent on them. According to a Harvard Business School case, during its first stage, called "Concept Review," "the marketing team conducted an assessment of sales based on data from comparable game titles, while the development team worked up a preliminary schedule and budget for the project. With these data available, the marketing team then established a rough-cut profit and loss (P&L) forecast for the title."[5] But they often found "comparable game titles" an unreliable guide to enduring special appeal. The marketing research on big hit *Tony Hawk* far underestimated its eventual success. *Mechwarrior 2*, one of the company's biggest titles ever, had been cancelled in its early project stages by management and went on to success only because rebellious game developers kept working on it after being told to stop. The problem: assessments of potential based on data from comparable titles, almost always on resemblance within broad or surface categories (other skateboarding titles, other 3D first-person shooters in space, and so on), take no account of the maker's efforts to create a unique and coherent form.

4

The problems with category comparisons that take no account of internal coherence are nowhere as apparent as in the movie industry. Consider the following.

During the summer of 1999, within a span of less than a month, three new horror movies landed in theaters. First, on July 16, came a fake documentary, *The Blair Witch Project*. Made for only $60,000 production cost ("a celebration of rock-bottom production values," according to critic Roger Ebert),[6] it opened on twenty-seven screens, exploded to more than a thousand two weeks later, and then to more than twenty-five hundred by August 20. Critics liked it and so did audiences; it ultimately grossed more than $140 million in the United States alone. Seen as a percentage of production costs, that figure made it one of the most profitable movies of all time.

One week later, on July 23, *The Haunting* opened. Based on Shirley Jackson's novel, and a remake of a film that earned a Golden Globe nomination for director Robert Wise in 1963, *The Haunting* featured well-known actors Liam Neeson, Catherine Zeta-Jones, and Bruce Dern. It opened on more than twenty-eight hundred screens but in four weeks had dropped to fewer than nine hundred. Though it ranked number one and grossed $48 million in the United States for its opening week, box office receipts fell by 50 percent or more in each of the next five weeks. Critics disliked the movie, panning it for a poor screenplay and for overdoing special effects. It garnered five "Razzie Award" nominations, including for Worst Picture, Worst Director, and Worst Screenplay. It cost $80 million for production and eventually earned a domestic gross of just over $90 million. Its worldwide gross of over $177 million kept it from being a financial disaster, but it certainly disappointed everyone.

Two weeks later, on August 6, a film we've already met, *The Sixth Sense,* opened on 2,161 screens; over the next six weeks, more theaters picked it up, as it became clear that this film "had legs." Even though it opened with slightly lower first week box office than *The Haunting*, $43 million, the take declined much more slowly, each week in the 10 percent to 20 percent range.

Eventually the movie's run extended to thirty-nine weeks, more than twice as long as *The Haunting*. *The Sixth Sense* collected six Academy Award nominations, including for Best Picture, Best Director, and Best Screenplay; it received four BAFTA (British Oscar) nominations, including for Best Film, Best Direction, and Best Screenplay; and it won the People's Choice Awards for Favorite Dramatic Film and Favorite Film. Its U.S. gross of more than $293 million on production costs of $40 million gave it a greater net than *The Blair Witch Project*.

Figures 4.1 and 4.2 show these movie releases across their first sixteen weeks in theaters.[7]

We lay out these comparisons to suggest that although these movies might appear to be similar products—horror films released in U.S. theaters the same summer—they are, in the ways that audiences reacted to them, quite different, though not for reasons that broad or surface category comparisons can explain.

Category comparisons in the movie business often rely on factors such as genre (horror), the prominence of stars (Catherine Zeta-Jones, Bruce Willis), or director. But these kinds of comparison provide little help in explaining people's different reactions

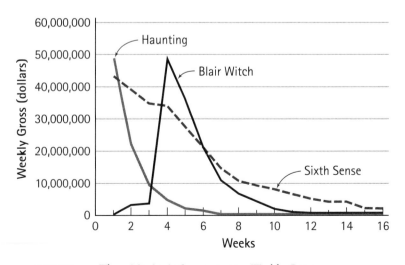

FIGURE 4.1. Three Movies in Summer 1999: Weekly Gross.

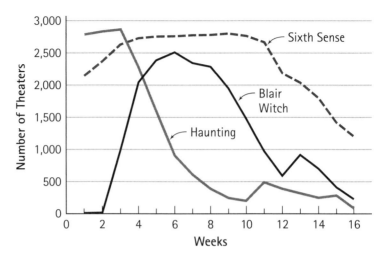

FIGURE 4.2. Three Movies in Summer 1999: Number of Theaters.

to these films. *The Blair Witch Project* had unknown stars and director; largely thanks to that fact, to marketers thinking about category comparisons (assessing the movie's potential sales by comparing it to other no-name horror flicks), it opened on very few screens. But its sales exploded. There was something about it that didn't enter in to the category comparisons of marketers.

Similarly, *The Haunting* and *The Sixth Sense* both had stars, but *The Haunting* had more, and its stars, especially Catherine Zeta-Jones, were considered bigger draws than the up-and-down Bruce Willis, the name in *The Sixth Sense*. Neither film had an especially prominent director (at the time—Shyamalan has since become quite well-known, or "bankable"). Thanks to analyses by marketers, who based their thinking on category compari-sons, *The Haunting* opened on over 600 more screens than *The Sixth Sense* and 2,773 more than *The Blair Witch Project*. Over the next few weeks though, *The Haunting* proved to have little audience appeal (and to suffer derision by reviewers), while the other two proved that there was something about them that au-diences (and reviewers) really liked.

5

We've briefly met movie industry researcher Arthur De Vany who, working with various coauthors, has thoroughly and scientifically analyzed returns in the movie industry. "We have been able to show," he reports, "that movie revenues follow a non-linear dynamics that bifurcates into two separate paths, one leading to long lives and high revenues and the other leading to brief lives and low grosses."[8] De Vany and his colleagues show that these differences result from an "informative" rather than "uninformative, information cascade."

When moviegoers look at how many people saw a movie last week, and use only that information to decide what to see this week, De Vany calls that an "uninformative information cascade": moviegoers as lemmings.

But that's not what happens. Moviegoers exchange information about what they thought about a movie, what they saw within it, and how they experienced what they saw. Word-of-mouth and other information (such as reviews and social media) about that special something within a good movie gets around and influences audience behavior more and more as the weeks pass. What happens to a movie's box office next week *does* depend on what has happened this week, but the nature of the dependency tips into one or the other of two categories—call them *hit* and *miss*. Once established as one or the other, the two kinds of "products" behave very differently. A hit's success *is* driven by past success, but nothing can save a miss from rapid descent into obscurity.

Maybe, we suggest, audience members make judgments on the basis of coherence, on the way the parts of a movie function together. People who see the movie reason out its unity of form, and they tell other people about it (though probably using feeling words, not our technical terms).[9] It's not the sheer numbers of people who "contemplate" such a product that matters. It's what people tell each other about their experience. What they think and feel about that experience has important influence on a movie's eventual commercial success, for better or for worse.

6

Sequels are an especially interesting part of this discussion of category comparisons. The decision to launch a sequel is usually a decision to construct a form with category similarities to one that audiences in the past found coherent. Audiences with a favorable subjective impression of the first movie go to the sequel in search of a similarly gratifying experience. Because the sequel is usually the result of a marketing exercise aimed at producing recognizable categorical similarities, however, audiences are often disappointed by it. Sequels behave more like *The Haunting*. People come at first, but they discover the sequel has no coherence, no soul. It superficially resembles the original, but it is not special in the same way that the original was. Figure 4.3 shows the pattern of sales for the *Blair Witch 2* sequel. It opened reasonably well then crashed as audiences discovered that it was not nearly so special as the original.

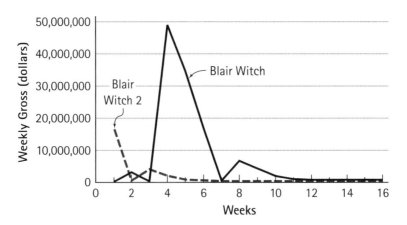

FIGURE 4.3. Sales for *Blair Witch 2*.

7

Sequels can be successful, and they often make money. But unless the same attention to coherence that characterized the original happens for the sequel, it will most likely not have the coherence of the original. Our notion of doublethink comes again into play: the sequel makers must treat the sequel as if it were an original. Otherwise, audiences or customers will find it disappointing.

It does happen that a sequel can have coherence. *Aliens*, directed by James Cameron, a sequel to *Alien*, directed by Ridley Scott, did well at the box office. Note that James Cameron isn't a director who coasts on the energy of a predecessor. He made his own movie, using materials that continued a story. The result of his work, though recognizably part of the *Alien* story, sharing one character and a venue, has its own style of plotting, its own resonant coherence.

Some companies do a good business on the basis of category comparisons, by alertly recognizing and following marketing trends. They may disappoint audiences with their products and services, but if sales open big enough, the business can still succeed. Sequels that open big then crash are not infrequently profitable (though they are never wildly so, not the way originals such as *The Blair Witch Project* or *The Sixth Sense* can be). Many businesses prefer this approach, which they consider lower risk than trying to make and market special things. When a video game company buys the rights to create a game based on a successful movie, they hope to capitalize on the audience's favorable impression of the movie for long enough to open big enough to make a reasonable profit. Occasionally the game makers produce something special through this kind of intellectual property licensing, but more often they don't.

Figure 4.4 distinguishes among two different (but non-exclusive) focuses a business might adopt (focus on coherence or focus

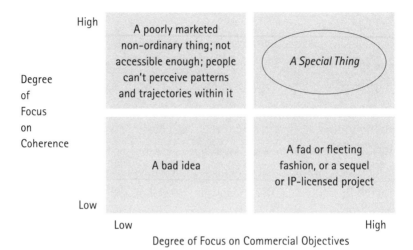

FIGURE 4.4. Possibilities for Business Focus.

on commercial objectives) and four different kinds of business outcomes.

Businesses that engage primarily in category comparisons that help them follow fads end up in the lower right quadrant, which represents a low degree of focus on coherence combined with a high degree of focus on commercial objectives. They often disappoint customers seeking to reexperience something special, but it's a lower-risk business than going for a new special experience, so this business model can work. The upper right quadrant is our focus in this book, however.

Pure artists, people who create art-for-art's-sake, congregate in the upper left quadrant. They rarely make much money. This quadrant also includes people who didn't know how to market a special product or service. We're not inclined to disparage anyone happily working on art for its own sake. But in this part of this book, we're particularly interested in (1) how one gets to the top row (makes coherent things) and (2) how one moves from the upper left to the upper right (successfully markets special things). These correspond to the two challenges we mentioned earlier.

Somehow businesses that aspire to make and market special things, that operate in the upper row, must create space for makers to differentiate their products and services on the basis of intrinsic quality and formal coherence. More than that, they must support and nurture the activities that lead to creation of coherent forms, even though doing so runs against their risk-averse inclinations to make category comparisons as a way to play it safe.

8

Though an up-and-coming firm in 2005, e-Types, a Copenhagen-based design firm we mentioned earlier, was not so well-established that it could count on an invitation to participate in major design competitions. So when Team Danmark (TD), the quasi-governmental entity that supports the country's athletes at international sports events (such as the Olympic Games and the European Championships) called on three Copenhagen design firms for proposals, e-Types managers and designers alike were delighted to be included. The winner would create the public face of the national sports teams, a very high-profile assignment. By winning the TD competition, e-Types could vault into the top tier of regional design firms.

From its beginning, the firm's designers had embraced an edgy sensibility, taking their name from labels for additives to food products in Europe ("e-100," for example, is a yellow-orange food coloring). The headline for a newspaper article announcing the firm's arrival called them "Ass-Kickers and Cowboys." Out of sympathy with current directions in design, e-Types aimed—in the words of its founders—to "smash the world."

Success came quickly. Tech startups inflating the late 1990s dot-com bubble needed plenty of help with design. When the bubble burst, e-Types merged with Wetware, a strategy consultancy with great connections in the (bubble-resistant) public sector. High-profile new projects began with Georg Jensen, Aarhus

Business School, and Aquascutum in London. The firm grew, hiring designers, project leaders, and an administrator.

The new partners from Wetware helped refine the e-Types business concept, expanding the firm into a full-fledged brand agency, ready to design a corporate identity, advise companies and other organizations on identity issues, position a brand, and formulate marketing strategy. They hired business-school-trained strategists who worked alongside designers to integrate the disparate parts of each client's identity and to distinguish clients from their competitors. The new approach attracted large new clients: Carlsberg Brewery and Levi Strauss, among others. And although e-Types developed a considerable degree of business professionalism, its core design staff retained that smash-the-world sensibility, differentiating their firm from others by way of exciting, edgy designs, all with (to use our terms, which they did not) a notably high degree of resonant internal coherence.

But the TD competition strained the company's sense of its identity. It offered less-than-ideal ground rules. The limited brief contained mostly visual guidance, not the rich background on strategy, goals, and thematic factors that e-Types staff had come to prefer. The contest brief called for an evolution, not a revolution, of the current identity, an imperfect fit with e-Types's edgy inclinations. Worst of all, the contest allowed only three weeks to prepare a proposal, not a lot of time. But the young design firm could not pass up such an opportunity to gain exposure.

Working directly from the brief, e-Types designers quickly developed an evolutionary proposal that everyone considered strong. Most people thought they had a winner; company experts estimated their probability of winning at about 80 percent. But then came a glitch: key designers, even those who had created the design, didn't like it. They considered it boring. They did *not* want to be known for this kind of work. A short time later, these designers produced an alternative design, one that they greatly preferred.

Not everyone at e-Types liked the new design. Those with business in mind, managers and strategists, raised questions. Would Team Danmark accept this edgy design? "It's the one *we like*," they argued, "not the one *they want*." Some thought the design too radical; everyone agreed that this design was less likely to win the competition, with maybe a 20 percent chance. But by now designers "hated" the first design. Opinions grew more heartfelt. Positions hardened.

Figure 4.5 contains excerpts from some of the points made on each side, recounted in interviews after the fact (often with noticeable heat).

After extensive debate, the e-Types partners agreed to show the client only the edgy design, the one the designers liked, even though they knew it would be unlikely to win. Speaking of the evolutionary design, Managing Director Søren Overgaard summed up the ambivalence: "We wouldn't really have liked them to choose it." And, as expected, e-Types did not win the competition.

Some business-trained staff members were unhappy about this. Some called the decision to go with the edgy design "unprofessional." They argued, in effect (to use our terms, which they did not), that both designs were coherent, but the edgy design was not accessible to the client and thus never should have been offered.

9

In the aftermath of the client's decision, though, the e-Types partners began to see the moment when they decided to go with the edgy design as the defining moment in the successful

The Designers' Perspective	The Analysts' Perspective
"It's impossible to make a design if we follow TD's rules....You can't [change the colors] because the colors are the red and white of the Danish flag; you can't add blue. You can make a beautiful torch, but you can't do anything with five rings locked together—that is a logo in itself."	"If you stay inside the client's limit, it's boring. But if we go too far outside the limit, the design is too crazy and it won't be realized. We have to find that magical place where TD will go a little further than they thought they could, but we don't take them so far out that they won't dare to cross the bridge."
"We did the classical design first and it's bad. So we took a chance to try something different, to get ideas out of doing something crazy. The classical design, it's not beautiful."	"If we want to win the competition we should show them both the classical design and the revolutionary one [and let the client pick—probably the classical design]."
"[The first design] is not a job from e-Types; it could be from anywhere. We shouldn't show it to anybody."	"How selfish do we want to be? When we talk to our clients, we say we want to help."
"The new design is a great design! It is true to what e-Types stands for. Maybe this is wrong for the client, but on the other hand the design could move TD in a great direction."	"It's possible that even if we lose the competition with the new design, we will earn 'integrity currency.' But how much cash flow currency can we sacrifice for respect [from other designers]?"
"Why win the competition and maybe earn a little money, but not that much, and make a thing that doesn't have any meaning for you? Every time it's on TV I'll be thinking, 'Oh crap, I did that.' It's like the medieval knights—it's not about money, it's about honor."	"This is a business. It's about money."

FIGURE 4.5. Excerpts from the Team Danmark Design Debate.

formation of the company's long-term strategy. The decision to present the edgy design was, they argued, fundamentally consistent with their desire to smash the world as a differentiated player of unusual integrity.

Two factors constrained their firm's ambition at the time of the Team Danmark decision: (1) limits on the amount of work the firm could take on, due to a shortage of key design talent and (2) customers' hesitation when asked to pay premium fees for their design services. Doing more work or charging more for the work they did—either would have been a route to improved commercial results.

Presenting the conservative design, the e-Types partners decided, would have worked against their interests in both these respects. To present the conservative design would cost them street credibility, which would prevent them from attracting other good designers like those already on staff. Presenting the conservative design would also diminish their reputation for differentiated output: as one designer complained, any design firm could do that design—it presented nothing unique to e-Types. Had e-Types presented the conservative design, it would have risked becoming famous for "the wrong kind of work," the kind of work the designers felt least capable of and least wanted to do.

Subsequent events vindicated the e-Types decision. Large, conservative clients began to approach e-Types when they wanted something more edgy than their usual fare. As hoped, these large clients with big budgets came asking for the kind of work e-Types most wanted to do, the kind of work they could do best. Overgaard gave an example: "A [large] pharma company we now work with noticed our cultural design stuff, and wanted that edgy quality. We don't have to sell out to move up in market—we would have been less interesting as a design company."

10

The Team Danmark episode at e-Types illustrates a point we heard emphasized again and again in research interviews: effective strategy for a firm that makes and sells special products means *saying "No"* to some business—to customers who will not let you take differentiation and coherence sufficiently into account, who won't allow you to work beyond their uninformed ideas of what they think they need. A firm that makes and sells non-ordinary products cannot afford a client that won't honor or can't appreciate these factors.

11

Overgaard described the immediate aftermath of what might have been perceived as a crushing loss of the Team Danmark job: "After the closure was made everyone was feeling 'Wow, we really say "No" and we're standing up for what we really believe in.' So this is actually quite a good feeling. Even though we lost, we know we've done the right thing."

This strategy succeeds, however, only if you can satisfy certain prerequisites. In our interview, Overgaard pointed out, "If you want to be a really great creative company, you have to have a certain amount of cash flow, so you can afford to say 'no,' so you don't have to do something you don't really believe in." Sufficient cash provides freedom to attend to plot, which in turn makes it likely that you'll get more cash (more of your special kind of business, for which you can charge higher prices). We saw this virtuous cycle, success feeding success, again and again in our research. In interviews from another case within our research project, we saw that Ascent Media's digital color effects artist Stefan Sonnenfeld benefited from a similar cycle. So did top video game studios that we also studied in our research. Cash can fund the maker's freedom, which, exercised, brings more cash.

This principle of strategy has implications, of course, for how you run your day-to-day business. Rasmus Ibfelt, another e-Types partner, explained his ambitions for the company, and some of their implications, this way:

I want us to get this position in the world, which is beyond reach. I want people to come . . . ask us to do the project and no one else because we are the only ones who can do it. And if we want that position, we cannot become established. Becoming established means that we will need to take in clients we don't really want to work for, because we need to feed the people, pay the salaries. . . . If the project is just somewhat interesting, and they can pay the fee, but it doesn't match, like, maybe the brand we have, what should we do? I think it is very, very important, now in these "successful" times, that we actually dare to turn people down, in order to use our efforts in the right area and on the right clients.

Ibfelt's view suggests a need to keep cash flows flexible. Doing that, in this kind of firm, can be difficult, because the biggest costs are salaries, which are hard to adjust. This strategy requires careful deliberation about adding staff, because each person added represents the possibility of pressure, during a period of slow business, toward taking jobs you'd rather not take. For e-Types, the fear of becoming "established" also influences *whom* they hire, how they make decisions about designs, and the shape of client interactions. Ibfelt also told us it meant that partners had to provide considerable latitude to younger designers who come in with fresh ideas.

12

In mid-2008, success yet again warmed e-Types. They had redesigned packaging for a major client, strategically repositioning the client's products, recasting them from a category sold alongside baby powder and toilet paper into beauty products. Competitor packaging employed a design approach best described as "shout as loud as you can," using all kinds of colors, widgets on the shelves, and other lurid tricks. e-Types had a different idea. "If everyone else is shouting," designers at e-Types reasoned, "then whisper." They toned down the packaging design and made it classier, more exclusive, taking cues from the world of cosmetics such as using white and gray with one strong contrasting color added. This worked very well. People at the client company appeared delighted.

Then, without warning, groups within the client's marketing organization launched a campaign against the new approach. They wanted to keep up the shouting and did not like the subdued style. At about the same time, the client appointed a new CEO, who sided with the marketers and ordered some changes to the design. e-Types designers, true to past form, fought this idea. Remember David Lewis's two centimeters: you can't change only some parts of a coherent design. Coherent designs have interdependent parts and patterns. Changing some parts of the packaging design would have required other changes—a complete reconceiving, in fact. The CEO's redesign order provoked in e-Types a crisis similar to the TD crisis. The partners looked back at their interpretation of what had happened in the aftermath of the TD decision—e-Types had attracted big clients who came looking for edgy designs. Only one choice seemed possible: they refused.

In effect, e-Types fired this client.

Then they suffered from bad timing. e-Types fired this big client in August of 2008. On September 15, 2008, in distant New York City, Lehman Brothers filed for Chapter 11 bankruptcy protection, which triggered what's now called "the financial crisis." Within weeks, credit lines for small companies dried up and design firm clients trimmed their budgets. Over the next year, demand for e-Types's services softened. In hindsight, everyone recognized August 2008 as a very bad time to fire a client.

The effects of the downturn and subsequent cash-flow issues put severe pressure on the e-Types strategy of saying "No" to business that reduced the firm's differentiation. Eventually, the partners faced a decision: lay off staff, or accept work the designers didn't want to do. They opted for layoffs, choosing the trauma of saying goodbye to close friends so they could preserve their principles as makers of special things.

Since that time, demand for their services has improved, and they've begun to recover. The managers still believe they made the right decision in opting for layoffs. More savvy about business cycles, however, they've since established a subsidiary company and separate brand, called "India," to do less differentiated "production work." Now, when e-Types says "No" to a client, India can say "Yes." The volatile, high-margin e-Types business is paired with the steadier, lower-margin India business.[10]

13

In firms we examined, staff debated this issue more or less constantly. Overgaard described a need to maintain *balance*:

[Design] is somewhere between art and consulting. . . . You strike a balance where you do something that the client couldn't ask for themselves, but at the same time it has to fit the client. You can't do something that's so arty or strange or so off the point that the client won't get it, or the clients that they have won't get it, because then you aren't really helping them. But that's a difficult balance. You have to respect the craft of the designer, but at the same time you have to respect the client, and get those two things to meet. I think that's the challenge of every creative company.

14

Evidence from our research interviews suggests that creative firms often think about growth differently from the way conventionally industrial firms do. Designers and other creatives we interviewed expressed clearly their lack of interest in "scalability." A business makes a scalable thing when it can replicate that thing exactly as many times as needed. This allows industrial firms to access economies of scale. But the creatives we interviewed had no desire to manufacture a zillion of anything.

Ptolemy, a metal sculptor we interviewed, has become famous for transforming automobile hubcaps and wheel covers into striking representations of fish, dragons, and other creatures. Not surprisingly, his work attracted the attention of automakers. On one occasion, he told us, an automaker offered him a commission to make dozens of identical sculptures from its wheel covers. When they began to discuss price, philosophies came into conflict. The auto company representative, consistent with purchasing behavior in normal industrial settings, asked for a volume discount. He argued that because Ptolemy would sell so many sculptures in a single transaction, he should share some of the benefits of this economy of scale with his customer and charge a lower price per unit.

Ptolemy vehemently disagreed. He would charge more per unit, he told the auto company rep, because he hated to make the same sculpture again and again. The job offered him not an efficiency benefit but a huge boring-work penalty. So Ptolemy proposed sharing that penalty with the buyer, by charging a higher price. As the only source for these sculptures (and probably because the amount of money at stake was not huge), Ptolemy prevailed.

Resistance to doing the same thing twice was a recurrent theme in our interviews. Many people within creative firms, when they thought about growth, thought not of replication but of *extension*. Often they talked about extending some core notion into other products and services that shared the firm's design "DNA."

Genetic theory distinguishes between *genotype*, the full but implicit encoding of genetic information, and *phenotype*, the observable forms and behaviors the genotype brings to life. No one we talked with used these terms, genotype and phenotype. But a lot of them had the idea that DNA (the genotype), while implicit and not observable, nevertheless determines an emergent form (the phenotype). In our terms, the genotype organizes the maker's thinking about how to make new unique and coherent forms. Some firms we encountered, driven by creative staff, aspired to make new forms that, by virtue of their coherence, created a group sensibility, a corporate culture, and a deep resemblance in the firm's outputs. Creatives we interviewed seemed especially to like the fact that DNA, the essence or engine from which new coherence can be generated, remains implicit, hidden, and they (usually) resisted any attempt to codify genotypes.

The implicit-ness of creative DNA has a couple of obvious implications for business strategy. It helps explain why coherent forms might be difficult to imitate. Only Vipp can make Vipp-like products. Other firms can't easily decode the DNA from which special things emerge, partly because it's not written down anywhere. You can't accidentally leave plot behind on a train for someone else to find, in a manual, or on a lost laptop's hard drive. Because there's no such thing. It's an idea, a way of working. And of course, if your competitor can't imitate your product, plan, or service, you have a significant advantage.

But the implicit-ness of this DNA has a downside, too. If the key value-generating aspects of a product or service are not explicit, neither are the steps you take to make one. You can replicate an industrial service—in a fast food restaurant, say—by carefully following explicit procedures. Other people can "read the manual" and take a class; many people can learn the key value-creating activities. But it's not nearly as easy to extend a special making activity. You can't create a unique thing by reading a manual, and you can't join a creative ensemble by taking a training class. Instead, you have to participate in and come to understand a constantly evolving collective frame of mind. You have to live with the other creators and absorb the sensibilities of their work and its outcomes (products, services, ideas); you have to "learn" the forms of their artful work and its emergent outcomes.

Creative firms depend, to a remarkable degree, on things like this DNA, which is embedded within and shared among certain key creative individuals. It's only natural then that we should worry about how to manage these key people who harbor the firm's design DNA.

15

In the restaurant business you can have a fast food joint or a Spago. Without Wolfgang Puck, there's no Spago. Without Stefan [Sonnenfeld, an in-demand "colorist" at Ascent Media], there's no Company3 [Sonnenfeld's studio and "brand"]. This business doesn't work without very high-end talent. We're not a fast food joint.

—Bill Soloman, president of Creative Services, Ascent Media[11]

It's common to portray so-called "creative individuals" as people whose inclinations and behavior put them at odds with conventional managers. Authors of research on creative industries have, for example, described creatives as men and women who reflexively resist or disregard economic, or indeed any external, motivation or rationale to justify their work.[12] Researchers have described creative people as a class as "nonconformist,"[13] or as rebels against efforts to direct them toward the manager's objectives.[14] We've described and quoted a few such people: David Lewis refuses to extend the chassis of a TV two centimeters to help solve a component supply issue; Jonas Hecksher, the creative director and a partner at e-Types, spoke eloquently about his firm's refusal to show Team Danmark the "classic" design because they weren't proud of it, even though he agrees that it had a better chance to win the competition than the design he liked best. Paul Robertson, mentioned in Part 1, doesn't "give a tosh" about commercial objectives in making his music, because, he says, "I'm doing it for me." Creatives earn their keep when they exasperate traditional managers by resisting actions that might compromise the purity of their plotting and its resultant coherence.

Traditional managers have never liked dependency on the creative individuals within their companies.[15] And who can blame them? These essential staff members differ extremely from those who work effectively within standardized processes to create value based on scale economies. Creatives may have little patience with traditional work methods, especially those that aim to chunk and routinize what they do. The managing director of a design firm told us how his company's designers relentlessly ridiculed and refused to comply with a financial bonus program introduced to recognize and reward good outcomes; managers had to end the program. We heard the chief scientist of a major pharmaceuticals company say, of the merit-based pay system imposed on the entire company by the board of directors, "I've finally gotten it to a point where it at least doesn't interfere with the work of my most creative researchers." Asked if that was the best he could say about his company's merit pay system, he paused thoughtfully, then nodded. "Yes, that's the best I can say about it."

This manager's partial success in bringing together two contradictory work conditions demonstrates that the perceived distinction between creative and manager, between creativity and management, while often real is just as often unnecessary. We spoke once with a novelist who became the provost of a college within a large state university. We asked him how, as a novelist, he reconciled himself to the job of administration. After a moment's consideration he said, "The thing is, I administrate with the same brains I use to write my novels." Let's look at an extended example of this principle in action.

16

Specialisterne ("The Specialists"), a Copenhagen-based company, provides software testing and some other services to a list of prominent international clients that includes Microsoft, Computer Science Corporation, Oracle, and Lego. Members of the company's consulting staff have skills uniquely suited to software testing and similar jobs: three out of four have been diagnosed with some form of Autistic Spectrum Disorders (ASD).

Autism is a brain condition that impairs social interaction and communication, and it leads those afflicted to exhibit restricted and repetitive behavior. The condition, which usually becomes evident before a child is three years old, poses significant developmental obstacles. But it can also include particular talents: exceptional focus, impressive thoroughness, strong memory. According to Specialisterne's founder, Thorkil Sonne, "Researchers have hypothesized, based on facts known about their lives, that many of history's great achievers—Albert Einstein, Socrates, Charles Darwin, and Isaac Newton among them—might have been afflicted by a mild form of ASD called Asperger's Syndrome."[16]

Sonne's inspiration to start the company originated when psychologists diagnosed his three-year-old son, Lars, as autistic. The condition presented the expected difficulties to Sonne and his family, but occasional surprises suggested that Lars possessed unusual capabilities. One day, for example, the boy began drawing a very elaborate diagram. At first, Sonne couldn't figure out what it was, but after a while it took on a familiar shape.

Gradually it became a map of Europe, but thick with perplex-ing numbers that meant nothing to Sonne. Later and completely by accident, as he looked through an atlas, Sonne stumbled on the source of his son's drawing: the index page. The numbers indicated pages in the book on which detailed maps of regions from the larger area appeared. This remarkable child had re-produced from memory the entire overall image, complete with numbering scheme, without a single error (Figure 4.6).

Sonne, who at the time enjoyed a successful career as an IT professional within a large telecommunications company, recog-nized potentially valuable capabilities in his son's behavior. To reproduce the diagram so accurately required a strong memory, the skill to concentrate on minute detail, and a willingness to submit to an exacting standard of accuracy. These mapped well on to the skills that Sonne looked for in software and system tes-ters. From this realization, he made up his mind to start a new software testing company in which the majority of employees would be people with ASD. To start the company, he quit his job and refinanced his home; he took a big risk, but he knew that to make a company that met and found value in the unusual needs of his employees would require his total attention.

Work done by disabled people, while providing a "social good," is sometimes price discounted, to reflect the likelihood of problems or additional overhead and expense. Sometimes the organizations in which such people work operate as charities or nonprofits. Sonne didn't want to go these routes. He made in-stead a for-profit company that offered a best-in-class service. He intended to pay industry-competitive wages and to train his employees to become the world's greatest software testers. Such a firm, he thought, could sustain itself and would genuinely ben-efit his special consultants; he would pay them to provide real value, not condescend to them with a handout. In effect, Sonne

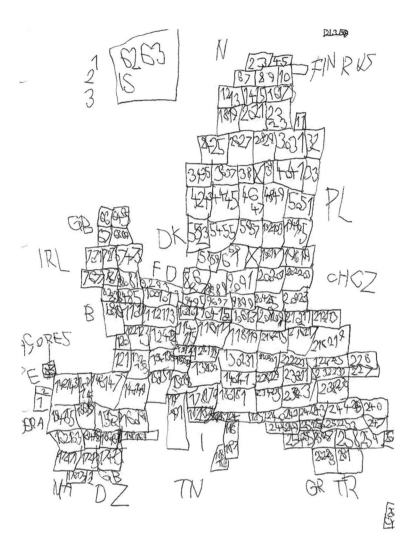

FIGURE 4.6. Diagram by Lars Sonne and Map (right) for Comparison.
Source: Thorkil Sonne; reprinted by permission.

reconceived the current ideas about disabled workers: instead of cramming them into conventional work situations, he made new workspaces, spaces that not only accommodated their special needs but set free (exploited, even) their special skills.

It was at first far from obvious that this could succeed. Autism can cause substantial impairment for those afflicted, notably in

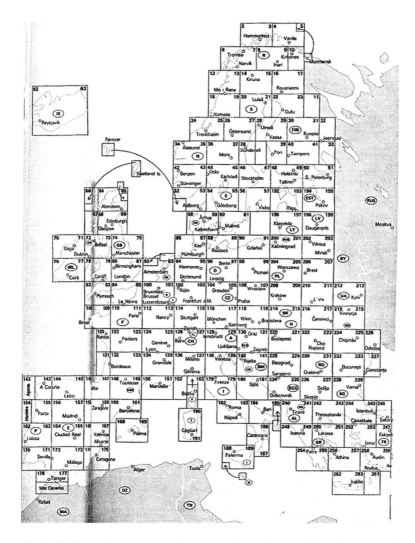

their ability to interact and communicate in social settings, and in social imagination. People with autism may appear aloof and indifferent; they often don't fully understand the meaning of common gestures, facial expressions, tones of voice, or irony.[17] In the United Kingdom, for one example, only 15 percent of adults with autism hold full-time jobs.[18]

Sonne aspired to move more people with autism into the "employed" category, to leverage their special abilities while he made a system in which their impairments could become strengths. On the basis of his research, he hypothesized that social interaction difficulties likely prevented many high-functioning autism people from acquiring and holding jobs. He believed he could overcome such difficulties in high-functioning autistic people. He designed support services to teach workers the job, invented work methods they could master, and designed social training to help them develop ways to interact with employers and colleagues. He made, in other words, places in which special people could work at peak levels of performance; produce genuine value; and, as a result, live productive, satisfying lives. And now, a few years later, it's become apparent that he was right.

How did he do it? The details are these: Specialisterne operational plans include a high level of support and careful handling for its special consultants. The company maintains an on-call response staff, people who can resolve issues that client companies don't know how to address. This support staff helps set up work situations that insulate consultants from the hectic, sometimes chaotic environment of the client and help to maintain the quiet, orderly work environment they need. Many can't work full time. Each presents a complex of particular mental conditions and a personal constellation of life difficulties. These all require special arrangements in the division of labor and the structure of each job. Sonne must include clients in the design process, persuade them to help make some unusual arrangements. Those who do usually find that it's worth it: the effort produces an impressive return. In other words, Sonne reconceived the idea of a software testing company, and made a new one. He's a poster child for the concept of manager as maker: he made workplaces, each one unique, where special things can be done. He conceived and made a business in which doing what comes naturally leads naturally to the desired outcome.

17

One of our colleagues, a senior business school professor who serves on the boards of directors for several large international firms, upon hearing the story of Specialisterne immediately raised an issue: "The thing that is hard to sort out is how much [additional] cost is being incurred by a customer to use these resources?"

Sonne, when asked why his company operates as a business instead of a charity, always highlights the skills of ASD consultants as a source of competitive advantage. He acknowledges that his consultants require extra support and extra management, but he also argues that they're worth it. The company estimates that their consultants are significantly more effective than traditional testing consultants, and that this more than offsets the cost of making a workspace in which ASD consultants can work effectively.

One reason to examine Specialisterne closely is that this kind of logic, which compares the benefits and costs of working with special employees to traditional models, applies in general when you're managing specially talented employees in ways that will, you hope, bring about outlier levels of performance. It's not limited to ASD consultants.

A manager at one of Specialisterne's client companies made this point eloquently. He told us that managing Specialisterne's ASD consultants had made him a better manager of all his staff. Managing ASD consultants, he said, required him to create the conditions needed to help them do their best. Work on that problem produced an epiphany for this manager. He realized that he could, and should, pay the same levels of attention to his other employees. Many of those, he observed, had eccentricities of personality or behavior. In the past, he'd regarded these differences as inconveniences he had to "put up with." After working with Specialisterne, he asked himself if he could find ways to make workspaces that could improve the performance of all his employees. Outlier behaviors can sometimes create coordination difficulties and additional costs, but this manager reckoned he'd have to cope with those no matter what. He was, he figured, already paying the costs of accommodating the eccentricities. Why not get some more benefit for his trouble?

This thinking and his performance represent a transition from the industrial dichotomy between manager and maker to a more artful notion of managers and creatives both as makers.

18

During a panel session at the 2005 Seattle Innovation Symposium at the University of Washington,[19] Frank Coker, president of Seattle-based Information Systems Management, Inc., described a similar transition in a tech startup:

One of my key players . . . really wants to be a [professional] musician. He quit [another well-known company where he made a fortune from stock options] and now he's working for me twenty to thirty hours a week. And what a deal I have! But I've got to be willing to let this guy go on the road, disappear for a couple of weeks at a time, go record CDs. But he does great work, so it's an opportunity. You've got to have some boundaries . . . but in general, I'm okay with this.

In the same session, Jonathan Roberts, founder of Ignition Partners (a venture fund), offered a related story:

I worked at Microsoft for thirteen years and had a chance to work on a lot of the great businesses there. . . . At the core of every product in these great businesses was a really great developer. These guys—no offense to them, but, well . . . they're all a little odd. So I developed a notion that [if you are one of these guys] you can extract a "tax" [an "oddness" cost] proportional to your degree of contribution. So if you are the core developer on a project, you can extract a pretty high tax. But you've got to isolate it from the rest of the team. And it can't get too high. I've had meetings with people where I've said, "Your tax is getting a little high."

This "tax" captured the extra cost of catering to special employees. Contributions from these employees make it worthwhile to pay the tax, as long as it doesn't get too high. Both these experienced executives treated the tax as part of doing business, an inevitable cost of management, and an opportunity to develop new methods. This "tax" is a really smart, but really industrial, way to account for the manager's creativity. Managers would do well to accept and exploit their creativity, to conceive of themselves as makers. They could, instead of addressing this tension with a dismissive label, include it as a potentially valuable part of the collaboration between themselves and a creative employee. They and the employee, both makers, could then become colleagues, collaborators rather than adversaries.

19

This idea applies our principles of making to an activity not usually conceived as creative. But in an innovation economy, idiosyncratic, special employees become the desired norm and managers must make the workspaces that allow them to do their best work. Managers who accept this new responsibility will see that a workspace can be a special thing, and that the principles of making we've outlined and reflected upon in these pages will apply to making and maintaining it. A workspace made of interdependent parts plotted to a coherence that achieves resonance becomes more than the sum of its parts; it becomes a special thing that will enable and support the makers for whom a manager made it. Within such spaces, each special employee presents a portfolio of skills and idiosyncrasies that is itself greater than the sum of its parts. Artfully managed, this portfolio creates value.

20

The Specialisterne corporate logo is a dandelion seed floating on the wind. As Sonne points out, the dandelion is a valuable plant. The leaves are edible and contain abundant vitamins and minerals. One cup contains 112 percent of a person's recommended daily quantity of Vitamin A. They are good sources of calcium, potassium, iron, and manganese—better than spinach. They contain beta-carotene; lutein; luteolin, an antioxidant; and zeaxanthin. Some say they promote healthy weight loss and liver detoxification. The flower petals can be used to make wine. Roasted and ground, the roots make a caffeine-free coffee. They're a natural diuretic, but also supply the potassium that other diuretics often cause you to lose. They reduce inflammation. There's some evidence that the leaves normalize blood sugar. They are important to bees early in the growing season, and they are food for butterflies. You can make rubber from *taraxacum kok-saghyz*, native to Asia and certain parts of Europe.

In the garden, however, or in your carefully cultivated lawn, you call the dandelion a *weed*. You don't want it, and you dig it up as soon as you can.

In the Specialisterne logo, the dandelion seed and its parachute represents Sonne's consultants, and it suggests the company's mission: to place those "seeds" in conditions where they can become valuable flowers. Don't squeeze them to fit in the molds and preconceptions that "neurotypicals" inhabit from day to day in an industrial idea of what it means to work effectively. Instead, make individual conditions that leverage the particular skills of each. Move the weeds from the lawn where they're not wanted and make them a place where they are wanted—by firms that seek to differentiate themselves in an innovation economy.

21

The manager who aims to get the best from the idiosyncratic skills of employees may experience a sense of role reversal. Whereas in a traditionally industrial hierarchy the worker does the bidding of the boss, in the arrangement we're suggesting, the boss becomes a facilitator for talented specialist workers. The manager steps into the background to plot and construct the workspaces others need. In addition, the manager may need to manage the disconnects—the logistical and timing difficulties that arise because staff members do their work in their own value-maximizing but idiosyncratic ways.

In many such settings, the manager labors under a handicap much more profound than any faced by his or her industrial colleagues. In the old days, a manager's job had rather simple boundaries. He or she (1) encouraged productive behaviors in employees, (2) discouraged unproductive behaviors, and (3) encouraged changes in behaviors when necessary. But the manager in an innovation economy firm, especially one that makes special things, isn't qualified to do this job. This manager may not understand what the most productive behaviors are at any given moment. And he or she cannot rely on being the first to see the need for an intervention or a change.

But this does not relieve managers of their main job: to make a workspace that can enable and encourage workers to create valuable things. Such a workspace permits them to control by release, to create a situation in which people doing what comes naturally leads to the desired end. Workers will still wander off the reservation or get out of synch with the organization's objectives. They'll disagree with each other and need help getting back together. Their manager must mediate such disputes. Moreover, managers of key creatives must manage without knowing, as their industrial predecessors often did, how to do the jobs they supervise. It's challenging work that often requires a light touch, variations in approach, experimentation, a willingness to bend, and a grasp of the shifting relationships among the parts of a project as they move toward arrangement in a coherent whole; a creative grasp, in other words, of plot, coherence, and resonance. The manager must move beyond technical mastery to—dare we say it?—artistry.

22

Managers must think a bit when they accommodate the desire of creatives to turn down uninteresting work. To do that often might leave them with too small a market. If your firm's sensibilities are very arcane, of the *Finnegans Wake* variety, say, then you may limit the size of your business by adopting this strategy, even if you provide special products and services. Some people, including many designers we spoke with in our research, considered size limitations a reasonable idea, if that meant they could do the kind of work they liked. Such a strategy obviously burdens a firm that wants to grow its business: it must meet a need to work hard to make its forms accessible, and must help its customers engage with patterns, discern trajectories, reason out the form, and learn to appreciate plot in the coherence of a non-ordinary product.

To "see" form, a person must recognize and engage with patterns that serve as the form's "beginning." If a person can't discern the pattern, or if the pattern doesn't carry with it some important associations, then he or she will never apprehend the suggested trajectories or form expectations about their resolutions. The form, no matter how coherent, will not generate that "Oh, wow!" event for this person, unless someone helps out.

This brings us to the second challenge for firms that make and sell special things, the marketing challenge.

23

In many design-oriented consumer product firms, the concern about making form visible to customers evolves into an obsession with how to display the product in stores and other venues (ad copy, websites, and so on). Vipp and Bang & Olufsen, for example, use a "shop-in-shop" concept: they take over a place in the store and remain in control of that area. Bang & Olufsen also employs, at considerable additional distribution expense, its own retail stores, where customers encounter only B & O products, arranged in exactly the way that the company thinks best.

These companies get very clever as they exert influence over how people experience their product even beyond the limits of company control. Vipp, for example, offers reporters press kits that include "story ideas" on disk, editable word processor files that a reporter on a deadline can cut and paste into his or her own document to get a quicker start on a story. These disks provide more than a dozen possible ideas, interesting stories that give readers patterns and associations they can use to appreciate a product's formal qualities and internal arrangements of parts and materials. Most reporters won't use the stories as is, but we suspect that many use Vipp's cut-and-paste docs as a starting point for writing a story, which gives Vipp influence, if not control.

Or, step in to an Apple store. You will find the products laid out so as to facilitate customer learning. Most who come have already experienced the "Oh, wow!" intuition and are eager to contemplate the special thing, to puzzle out its form and explore its usefulness. The thing is right there for them to play with, and there's a cheerful, suitably nerdy person nearby in a blue shirt ready to help out.

This type of influence has its limits. How and whether spectators can engage with patterns, or see trajectories and form, depends on what else they already know. We've mentioned the way people bring their own categories to the beginning of any experience. Arthur De Vany notes another kind of customer baggage that influences marketing strategies for movies. Audiences have seen other movies. Did those movies whet appetites for more, or create a desire for something different? After a decade of antiheroes, the good-versus-evil stories of *Star Wars* and *Raiders of the Lost Ark* felt refreshing, even if they recalled earlier formula pictures. Having seen certain forms, you may be more able to discern patterns and trajectories within other, newer forms.

When companies acknowledge that they have imperfect influence on an audience's ability to engage with a coherent form, the conversation often turns to timing: whether the "time is right" to introduce a special product or service. This is, of course, a judgment call. It depends on knowledge of how audiences have experienced things already on the market. This dubious conversation can easily slide down a slippery slope into an even more dubious conversation (If the thing is new, what can you compare it to?) about specific features of movies that might be "hot" or "cold." A statement such as, "Asteroids-smashing-the-Earth movies are really hot right now," moves dangerously close to a category comparison prediction. This sort of logic is often dominated by apophenia (seeing connections and sensing abnormal meaningfulness) and pareidolia (seeing something distinct and recognizable in vague imagery). We discussed these in more detail in Part 2.

24

In today's work atmosphere, filled with social media, there may be fresh ways to educate customers or to make them ready to see the coherence of a form before they buy. *The Blair Witch Project* was notable for its word-of-mouth-based prelaunch marketing strategy. Its marketers acted as if it was a genuine documentary.

They created a website where people could report discovery of footage supposedly filmed by a mysteriously missing film crew. Using elements of the movie's story, they built up the number of people who learned about, believed in, and engaged with the initial (fictional) premise, before the movie hit the theaters. The marketers cleverly arranged to have potential customers themselves seek out and find the information that would engage them in the movie before they saw it.

25

De Vany notes that no movie that has won an Academy Award for best picture or best screenplay has opened on more than fifteen hundred screens in the United States.[20] That means that most of these films, while original and coherent, didn't fit into conventional categories and that movie execs had limited confidence in their prospects. Because of the persistence of uncertainty, managers in a business that aims to make and sell special things—who don't want merely to play it safe by fast-following trends, licensing intellectual property from comic books, or making endless sequels—must have a way of managing the tensions of not being sure that customers will see coherence and experience resonance while contemplating a special thing. To do this, they must learn two important behaviors: (1) to think in portfolios and (2) to adapt rapidly as they learn more about how customers experience a product.

A manager who thinks in portfolios doesn't put all the eggs in one basket. A video game house will invest in some original concepts, some sequels, some tie ins. That is, its managers play it safe in part of their business, but not in all. Recall that e-Types now has the India brand to help it manage creative risk. A manager must tune the mix to acceptable levels of risk and return. As in most businesses, more risk (large number of coherent, original products) might produce more return (possibility of big success).

To best use the second approach, rapid adaptation, marketers find ways to learn in detail about customer responses and to
direct increased marketing efforts toward the positive and away
from the negative. "The only way to succeed in [the movie] business," says De Vany, "is to experiment and adapt."[21]

26

Our emphasis on nurturing makers and attending to their desires
to create original and coherent forms appears to leave out one
party often presumed important in business—the customer. In
recent years there's been increasingly excited talk about "crowdsourcing," which involves the customer in creation of a new thing.

Sony Pictures released the animated short feature *Live Music* in late 2009. The production developed what its promoters
call "the largest global animation collaboration ever."[22] Mass
Animation, an online studio, used Facebook to organize the
more than 50,000 fans from 101 countries who joined in creating the computer graphics that made the film. Over 17,000
people downloaded the free animation software provided on
the Mass Animation Facebook site. In the end, 124 groups and
individuals contributed scenes. Facebook fans voted for their
favorites, and an international jury of experts made selections
from these. Mass Animation took over the final cut. Fifty-one
animators from this crowd won $500 each and got their names
in the credits. Mass Animation attracted a global workforce of
self-motivated creative talent, generated professional content
without studio overhead, and potentially provided, according
to director and producer Yair Landau, a view of "the future of
creative collaboration."[23]

Live Music might seem to present a stiff challenge to our
notion of coherence as created by particular makers. When individual scenes were submitted for *Live Music*, there was no

reason for them to be coherent with each other, since they arose independently.

But before they invited the crowd to join in, creatives at Mass Animation had already plotted the story, dialogue, and soundtrack for the film.[24] They made the first scene to set the movie's style and look. In that process they designed the setting, drew the characters, and modeled their movement. This established a beginning, materials from which the middle and end would develop. The producers opened the process for a short time only, from November 17, 2008, to January 30, 2009. Content contributors picked scenes to work on and stayed within the already-plotted boundaries. While producers remained almost invisible during this time (with the exception of "jurors" on the Facebook discussion page to whom animators could write for help), the plot structure enforced by Mass Animation acted as a strict control over outcomes, ruling out the possibility of any ideas or discoveries that would require Mass Animation to reconceive their original design. Landau made final cuts, and Mass Animation (with Reel FX) worked with studio animators to edit and refine scenes for consistency.[25]

In effect, this movie *was* crowdsourced, but the producers and director did the plotting. Here is the resolution, then, of the concern that user-centered approaches and coherence might not be compatible, or that crowdsourcing might not be a way to make special things. The two ideas can be combined to valuable effect, *provided someone has the job of plotting the unity necessary for coherence.*

It need not be a single person. Teams and ensembles collaborate every day, using long-refined practices to create coherent outcomes. A theater ensemble will make a version of *Hamlet* never before seen, using an approach in which individuals (actors and director) use material drawn from each others' work,

constantly reconceiving the emerging play with a common purpose of plotting it more coherently at each iteration. Coherence
arises from group process. The director guides and suggests,
then makes choices among the alternatives created by the group.

27

There are many ways to make a coherent thing, and many ways
to help the audience perceive pattern, trajectory, and form.
Though the maker of special things must protect her or his process from influences (such as category comparisons) that work
against coherence, there's no particular reason that information
about customers, or the customers themselves, can't enter into
the work. They just can't be allowed to overrule choices that
lead to coherence.

In the end, managers will move toward commercial success
with special things as they learn to develop and nurture plotting
that achieves coherence and produces resonance among interdependent parts. Managers need to recognize that special things require special makers. Creatives may routinely do things and have
ideas that their manager cannot control in any conventional sense.
Outlier performance often demands outlier work conditions, difficult but essential to make and maintain. A manager must grasp
the principles (plot, coherence, and resonance) of special creation,
but may not have technical mastery over the actual work.

Creative marketers can then devise and implement methods
that enable customers to intuit, contemplate, and reason out
the form of a special thing. The natural pleasure derived from
this process can incline customers to buy and use a new, special
thing. Of course, no action can guarantee commercial success.
"Nobody knows anything!" applies to markets well beyond the
movies, but our research shows that special things, while unpredictable, or (like *Finnegan's Wake)* difficult to apprehend, have
a good track record.

PART FIVE

I

Some fifty years after its debut, *Kind of Blue*, by trumpeter Miles Davis and his quintet, remains the best-selling jazz album of all time. As we write, in the fall of 2011, it sells more than five thousand copies per week. But it didn't start out as a booming success. Dave Brubeck's *Time Out*, released in the same year, 1959, sold better than *Kind of Blue* at first. It's a special thing too. But *Kind of Blue* has won out in the long run.

Unlike the frenetic bebop that had made Davis famous, *Kind of Blue* is mellow, really mellow, a completely different kind of thing. Having taken bebop as far as he could, Davis knew he needed to try something radically different. The new thing had to be something he could do well. The great bebop trumpeter Dizzy Gillespie had mentored Davis, but Davis saw early on that he would never equal Gillespie's technical chops. Gillespie could play at tremendous speeds and reach high notes no one else even attempted. Davis couldn't come close. When Davis joined Gillespie's ensemble, he often refused to play the most technically challenging passages, insisting on leaving those to Gillespie.[1]

But Davis's shortcomings as a player didn't keep him from eventually eclipsing his more capable master. While with Gillespie, Davis fashioned musical ways to use rather than suffer his limitations; he developed a style (perfect for the later modal jazz) in which he played fewer notes, emphasized phrasing and rhythm, avoided vibrato, and stayed in the horn's middle register. Within this style, Davis began to improvise solos that had a new coherence, solos that produced effects greater than could be predicted from his skills. Gradually he became, as fellow band member Julian "Cannonball" Adderley would later put it, "not a good trumpet player but a great soloist."[2]

Davis turned to *modal jazz*—music in which the players organize their improvisations on scales rather than on conventional chord progressions and harmonies. Modal plotting produces an open, almost meditative sound, as neither ordinary chord progressions or conventional thirty-two-bar length constrain the improvisations.

Davis's modal jazz improvisations on *Kind of Blue* didn't involve playing higher or faster than others. He didn't drive any measurable indicators to higher levels of performance. In his new style he didn't develop a new capacity to do *more* of anything than he'd done in the past, thereby improving his "productivity." He invented a new style, with its own internal coherence. Within that style, he composed pieces that, while individual, had noticeable family resemblances.

Not everyone had an "Oh wow!" reaction to this new approach when it first appeared. Some early reviews described the trumpet playing on *Kind of Blue* as "morose," "maudlin," or "sluggish and low in energy output."[3] It took a while for some people to adjust, to appreciate how different the album was from what had come before it, how new, and to realize the musicality of what Davis and his quintet had done. By all accounts, Davis cared little for what critics thought and made no special effort to guess what customers would buy. He simply made music.

But this new conception made good sense to discerning listeners. As part of the liner notes on *Kind of Blue*, Bill Evans (pianist in the quintet) wrote an essay called "Improvisation in Jazz."[4] In it, he compares the music making on the album to a form of Japanese painting that requires the artist to make a picture by laying down a sequence of single, uninterrupted strokes, a method so direct that "deliberation cannot interfere." He notes that pictures painted this way "lack the complex composition and textures of ordinary painting," but that this technique nevertheless captures something "that escapes explanation." In our terms, the energy of the brush strokes as they interact creates resonance: the sequence of single strokes becomes a whole greater than the sum of those strokes. It is this same urge toward a "direct deed" as the "most meaningful reflection," writes Evans, that inspired the improvisations of *Kind of Blue*. The result, he argues, is something closer to "pure spontaneity" than anything else you could experience in a music performance. As Evans summarizes, an "improvising musical group needs its framework in time. Miles Davis presents here frameworks which are exquisite in their simplicity and yet contain all that is necessary to stimulate performance with a sure reference to the primary conception."[5] These are statements about the way the parts of a thing fit together into a whole. About intrinsic, not extrinsic criteria. About plot, coherence, and resonance.

Many people who come to *Kind of Blue* for the first time have an insight: "Oh, wow! This sounds great!"[6] Then, in contemplation, the music begins to insist on its newness, its difference from traditional jazz forms. None of the usual chord progressions appears to lead its musical ideas to closure. And yet, as you listen, a coherent form unmistakably emerges. Your contemplating mind instinctively searches for an organizing principle, for patterns you know, even if you can't name them. Most people will find these. A musician will quickly identify the modal scales of medieval church music. A layperson, a mere music lover, will not have the knowledge to make that identification, but will hear and "get" some of the patterns. This will provide a foothold. The coherence of the music is so strong, and the music so elegant in its open movement, that finally you don't need technical knowledge to appreciate it.

Recognize two patterns, and you have the beginnings of trajectory. You can begin to develop expectations, even though the principle of organization here is different from what you might know from past musical experience. You gain experience, even as you reason out the form. The trajectories arise first from antecedents outside the thing itself, the medieval modal scales. Beginning patterns imply middle trajectories, which move toward closure at the end.

Earlier, with the song "Three Blind Mice," we showed how repetition created patterns and trajectories that led through expectations to satisfaction at closure. The form of the little song, on the page, has affective significance, the potential to excite affect in a singer or listener. We hope you saw the coherence of this simple form. As a child you probably felt its resonance. And its lengthy history testifies to the power of that resonance in venues quite different from your mom's lap at bedtime.

Kind of Blue may seem at first different from "Three Blind Mice," but with a bit of contemplation you'll learn that they differ in degree, not kind. When "Three Blind Mice" concludes, you know that it is Baby Bear right. We presented some contemplation of that rightness and, we hope, increased the sense of that rightness in your appreciation of the song. When *Kind of Blue* begins, you should immediately feel that something's up, that something special's going on here. You'll be struck by the sound: spare and cerebral, yet lush, gorgeous, and rhythmically interesting. A knowledgeable musician will understand quickly what that something-up is: the change from standard chord progressions to modal scales as plot for improvisation. As a listener you may never need that insider knowledge to "learn" the "rules" of this unfamiliar musical form and begin to experience its resonance, its larger-than-the-sum-of-its-parts influence on you. When the beginning materials repeat to end a piece, you're very likely to get that satisfying Baby Bear sense of "Juuust riiight." You may never find out the technical details of why the music gets you, but each time you listen to it it'll get you again, maybe a little bit more, as you build categories to support your recognition of its patterns and trajectories, and learn to conceive increasingly sophisticated expectations about their direction and closure.

As you engage this special thing, this music, and think about it, perhaps you will conceive parallels and similarities between this experience and the processes of the kinds of making needed for special things. Your assignment, and we hope you accept it, will be to make a workplace in which other creative makers do things you don't understand, but that you must guide to closure. Miles Davis does not play world-class piano, but he makes an occasion in which Bill Evans can do his own best work.

What if you conceive your project as if it were a piece of music, with yourself as lead maker? What if you use memory and imagination to perceive and plot its patterns, trajectories, and repetitions? What if you understand and influence its organization into a beginning, middle, and end that together achieve a proper unity and magnitude? What if you plot the workspace, the work, the workers, and the emerging product into a coherent whole that has resonance beyond the sum of its parts?

These aren't rules for managing or making, they're ideas, ideas in the sort-of-Platonic sense we introduced earlier, directions for new thinking that can guide you as you and your fellow makers create the unique processes needed to make each special thing.

2

In these reflections, we've presented examples of high-end consumer electronics, graphic design firms, movies, stories, plays, songs, and so on. You no doubt have your own examples. In your business you may be eager to create special things with legs, upper-right-quadrant material as per Figure 4.4. Think of the variety possible in this quadrant. Think also of the different timelines you may want to use; legs by definition take a while to display themselves. Artful marketing of special things may help to reduce the time it takes for these legs to stretch out and to carry you commercially. Managers in a business that makes and sells special things need ideas they can use to think about the potential of special things as they move into the market. We've presented some such ideas; you'll develop your own as you work. Properly used, such ideas can begin and advance conversation about a special thing, not shut it down by freezing the special thing in a category left over from an industrial frame of mind.

Here follow a few thoughts for a maker of special things to keep in mind; takeaways, but not instructions you can use to solve particular problems. These are ideas; you can use them as material for creative thinking and doing.

3

Most human beings take pleasure in learning, in figuring things out. This is a major part of the appeal of special things: the task of puzzling out the form of a thing you've intuited as special.

4

Each individual person must conceive the form of a special thing. First, there's an event, a person's intuition, a nearly unconscious recognition of something special—an "Oh, wow!" moment. This event urges the person to contemplate the thing, puzzling out and learning (conceiving) the arrangements of its parts into a coherent form. These arrangements include the form's affective significance, which when realized in the pleasurable experience can often lead to new intuitions, new energy for further contemplation.

5

Each special thing is special in its own way, one of a kind. That means there are no formulas for making special things. Each time out you must solve the puzzle of fitting the parts together into a coherent whole. You can't get coherence by optimizing the parts individually, then gluing them together. If one part changes, the other parts must change to preserve the coherence of the whole.

6

Plot, coherence, and resonance govern the form of any special thing. And finally, a special thing includes everything that contributes to it: the company business plan and DNA, the décor of the in-store-display, the advertising, everything. Each of these, and all of them together, become the form of the special thing, and require care in plotting.

7

Plot is not a thing; coherence isn't quantifiable; and resonance keeps the secret of its power. These are all qualities that special things exhibit by virtue of being made by human agency. When a thing exhibits pattern it may be natural, like the rhythmic surf, but when a maker *arranges* the patterns into trajectories, and the whole becomes a unified, coherent thing, it then displays the quality called plot, the quality we've called the soul of design.

8

A special thing made for sale isn't a work of art, but it's enough like one that you can discuss and think about it using language and ideas developed to discuss and think about works of art.

9

Your reaction to a thing is not part of the thing.

10

Special things require, first and foremost, that marketers teach potential customers to perceive their form, and thus their coherence. If customers can't perceive the form, they can't experience the first pleasures of special things, recognition and learning. Special things achieve commercial value in part because of the pleasure associated with "reasoning out the form," the contemplation of a form intuited but not yet known. Marketing for special things needs to provide materials for intuition, and then help in the contemplation process.

11

Marketers help to create value by "educating" the market to see patterns, trajectories, and the repetitions that make them. These recognitions by a potential end user can end in sales, in commercial value. But no one can, on experience of the form, predict that value.

12

Timing matters. Sometimes the market isn't ready to see a particular form, or experience a particular plot, and no amount of educating will get them to where you want them to be. Many people didn't "get" *Kind of Blue* right away. People must first have other experiences, form other associations, before they can experience your special thing as special. We think of this as a potentially rich field for study and imagination: how to reconceive marketing for the long term.

13

A distinction between managers and creatives isn't always useful. It may be more productive to conceive of both as makers.

Managers make workspace, creatives design products and services. Others—craftsmen, engineers—bring designs to physical realization and complete the "cause" Aristotle called the efficient cause, or maker.

14

You need outlier performance from top creatives, not average performance. Creative businesses count on the last 2 percent, or last 0.5 percent. Those two centimeters on the back of the TV do matter. Matter? They're everything.

15

A company that makes and sells special things must sometimes say no and refuse a job of work that can't be special.

16

Painful choices within a job often require the company or designer to reconceive the whole project. Coherence doesn't brook "splitting the difference." For the creative who makes a special thing, compromise is not an option, so don't expect it.

17

When you make a special thing the customer isn't always right. The limits of the customer's imagination must not be allowed to limit yours.

18

Your imagination can, must, be an important tool for making.

19

Remember the dandelion principle: make a workspace in which other creatives can flourish. In the right conditions, dandelions are flowers. In the wrong conditions, they are weeds. You, as manager, make the garden.

20

Even when you're making a crowdsourced special thing, some maker has to worry about plot, coherence, and resonance—to conceive the necessary unity. This need not be a single person; collaborative teams are very good at achieving closure on complex special things (such as a play production).

21

Coherence does not arise from increasing the amount of anything good you're doing. It is not a consequence of "high performance" or "execution to plan." It's how a thing fits together, how the parts of a thing combine to make a whole that's greater than their sum. When you achieve it, people experience a thing powerfully. Sometimes they begin to speak of transcendent experience. But transcendence is a result, not a technique. Humble, skilled, dedicated work by all the makers (managers, designers, craftsmen) fits parts together in a plot unique to a particular special thing. That special thing might foster transcendent affect, but properly done the work stays earthbound.

22

A kind-of-Platonic idea, a guide for making and thinking about making, may have mutually exclusive features that cannot be resolved. Magnitude, for instance, requires that a thing be as big as possible and as small as necessary. The proportions differ for each special thing.

23

A valuable idea may also contain a counterintuitive tautology. Don't be put off by tautologies; they often contain serious wisdom. For instance, the final cause (reason for being) of a special thing is to be that particular special thing. At first glance this seems obvious; at second and third glance it leads to productive thinking.

24

There are many reasons for moving toward a creative economy; implacable changes in the global distribution of work and workers insist on it. The movement called "outsourcing" inevitably produces offshore manufacturers to supplant onshore industry in developed economies, by making things less expensively than firms based in those developed economies can. The threat of the insurmountably cost-advantaged offshore brand is real. When it starts to appear, making and selling special things may be the only viable way for some firms to survive.[7]

25

You *can* manage and make special things, even if you *can't* reduce the process to a formula or write a set of requirements for the team. The pessimists who think that economic urges always crowd out creative or artistic ones are dead wrong. In our research, we've seen example after example of creative makers working together, getting the balance right. If this is the business you want to be in, and we think it's a good one, you can do this too.

26

Good luck.

REFERENCE MATTER

GLOSSARY

This is not a dictionary, and these are not definitions in general use. Consider these words as terms of art used by us in this book, and, we hope, by you as you think about, make, and market special things.

ABDUCTIVE The notion that things reveal their purpose only through the unfolding of events. According to Charles Sanders Peirce, processes that aim to understand the second final cause, value, must be abductive.

AFFECTIVE SIGNIFICANCE The structural potential, intrinsic to the thing, to create affect.

ANTECEDENTS Materials from before that are similar to those you're presently considering.

ANTICIPATION The structural impetus toward a future. This is not an action by you, but a feature of plotted materials.

APOPHENIA To see connection or pattern among random data and ascribe meaning that isn't there.

BACK A relationship of similarity between the focus of your attention and its antecedents.

BEGINNING, MIDDLE, END   In *Poetics*, Aristotle's scheme for considering the unity created by the repetition of parts of a tragedy. A beginning has nothing before it, a middle and an end after; a middle has something before it and something after it; an end has something before it and nothing after.

CATEGORY   A mental box to put an idea or product in so as to collect similar things.

CATEGORY COMPARISONS   A crude way to predict (You hope!) the success of one thing on the basis of the success of something in the same or a nearby category.

CLOSURE   The resolution of trajectory and completion of form.

Simple closure: The ending satisfies your expectations.

Complex closure: The ending surprises your expectations, but on reflection appears more appropriate and more interesting than they were. Romeo and Juliet die, even as you hoped they would survive; but shortly you see that they couldn't have lived, based on who they were, what they wanted, and what they did. And this is dramatic structure, not psychology.

COHERENCE   A quality exhibited by a well-plotted non-ordinary or special thing. The interdependent parts of such a thing achieve coherence on the basis of plotting. A coherent arrangement produces resonance among its interactive parts.

CONCEIVE AND RECONCEIVE

Conceive: To make in imagination a coherent thing out of data and other materials; as when you contemplate a special thing to puzzle out, conceive, its form.

Reconceive: To take in new material and in combination with your own material, make or think up a new thing.

CONSEQUENCES   The structural result of arranged action, thought, or other material; a relationship of similarity with antecedent materials.

CONTEMPLATION   The process of puzzling out (conceiving) a special form; discovery of the parts and their plotted inter-relationships.

CRAFTSMEN   The persons, male and female, who realize designs in materials.

CREATIVES   Men and women presumed able to make new things; or to connect (unify) disparate ideas. Top-down management assumes (creates?) an adversarial relationship between managers and creatives. In this book, we assume that all makers (managers, designers, craftsmen) are creatives.

CROWDSOURCING   Involving a large number of customers (a "crowd") in creation of a new thing.

DNA   A metaphor from biology for a presumed implicit inner "code" that generates the form of a company and its products, and their familial relationships.

FEELING WORDS   Language we use to identify inner actions that we can't describe. Feeling words tell, for example, about the "Oh, wow!" moment of intuition.

FORWARD   The relationship of similarity a pattern projects over possible futures or extensions in space (or both).

FOUR CAUSES   Aristotle's comprehensive description of any made thing: why the thing is the way that it is.

Efficient cause: The energy that causes materials to become something they wouldn't become naturally (that is, a maker or makers).

Material cause: Those materials.

Formal cause: The ultimate shape (in space and time) of the new made thing.

Final cause: The reason for making the thing in the first place. Special things have two final causes: to be perfect and to create value (for example, commercial value in a business).

IDEA   The thing conceived virtually to a perfection unattainable in reality; often has mutually exclusive features; serves as a guide or template for thinking about and making special things.

IMITATION   A thing made of materials that don't make that thing without human intervention: a tree made of toothpicks, for example, or a smile made of paint.

INTERDEPENDENT   When the maker has plotted the parts of a special thing in tight relationship with each other, such that a change to one results in or requires changes in all the others. For example, asked to add two centimeters to the depth of a TV chassis, David Lewis redesigned the whole thing, changing almost every dimension.

INTRINSIC   Situated within the thing itself. For example, unity is an intrinsic quality of a non-ordinary thing; nothing outside the thing contributes to its unity.

INTUITION   An event in which one first apprehends a special thing in its entirety; the "Oh, wow!" moment. You know that thing is special, and you feel strongly about it, but you don't yet know why.

LEGS   When a product continues to create value for a long time. *Kind of Blue*, a best-seller for fifty-plus years, has serious legs.

MAGNITUDE   A thing's appropriate size and complexity.

MAKER   The human energy source that arranges materials into made things.

MANAGER   The maker primarily in charge of creating a workspace conducive to making special things.

NON-ORDINARY THING   A product plotted to achieve coherence with the accompanying resonance.

OBJET D'ART   A special thing made to only one final cause: to be perfect.

PAREIDOLIA   To see something recognizable in vague imagery; for example, the man in the moon.

PARTS   Components of a made thing.

Quantitative parts can be removed or shifted without essentially changing the thing; for example, the cap on a Coke bottle.

Qualitative parts, qualities, inhere in the thing itself, and can be removed or shifted only in imagination, such as the sexy curves of a Coke bottle. Note the unsuccessful efforts to make a bigger-than-six-ounce Coke bottle.

PATTERN   A sequence that repeats material from within itself or from elsewhere with a recognizable design based on a rule or convention.

PLOT   In Aristotle's *Poetics*, the principle that organizes all the parts and qualities of a tragedy; he called it the soul of tragedy. This is the quality a special thing has of being arranged. Plot is not a thing, like a book page or a cup handle, but a quality, like color, or length, or coherence. We call it the soul of design.

REALIZATION   The moment of closure in a plot sequence.

RESONANCE   A metaphor from physics; the mysterious increase in magnitude achieved by coherent plotting of a non-ordinary thing, in which the thing appears greater than the sum of its parts because of the way their harmonic interactions reinforce each other.

RULE   The plot principle for a pattern. The rule for the pattern 2, 4, 6 is "counting by twos."

SELF-REFERENTIAL   Construction organized by the thing itself. Its parts relate and refer to each other, not to the world outside it or an independent standard.

SOUL   Of special things, the underlying principle of organization; plot.

SPECIAL THING   A non-ordinary product that has a second final cause: to create value.

TAUTOLOGY   A statement in which the conclusion is the same as the premise, making it appear redundant and useless; for example, "The final cause of a special thing is to be that special thing." In thinking about art and design, tautologies often create opportunities for insight otherwise unavailable.

TRAGEDY   A kind of dramatic performance, a play. Aristotle used tragedy as the chief example for his book about making. This was probably the most complicated made thing he and his readership knew. Tragedies were the central feature of an annual holiday in Athens and other Greek cities that celebrated religion, sex, international trade, and politics.

TRAJECTORY

The directions in space and time proposed when two or more patterns relate to one another.

Shadow trajectory: directions in space and time that function beneath a larger, more evident arrangement of patterns.

UNITY   The condition in which the parts of a made thing have a relationship of repetition or similarity to other parts; for example, the sentence that begins and ends *Finnegans Wake*. It would be hard (impossible?) to count the number of times the key words of that sentence are repeated in the huge text.

WORKSPACE   The venue, created by a manager, in which others can make special things. Ideally, a manager plots a workspace to exhibit the qualities of a special thing.

CASES EXAMINED

Listed here are the cases we examined in our study. As permitted by the arrangements made with case subjects, some of these are identified in the text and in this list; others are not.

CASE NUMBER	CASE DESCRIPTION
1	Bang & Olufsen: High-end consumer electronics core design team
2	Drug development team in a pharma company
3	Medical device development team in a pharma company
4	Vipp: High-end bathroom products core design team
5	e-Types: Core creative team within a small graphic design firm
6	Elite process improvement team within a large aerospace firm
7	Downstream product team within an aerospace manufacturing plant
8	Service delivery team in a fast food restaurant
9	Project team within a product design firm
10	Ascent Media Group: Digital effects team within a large media company

CASE NUMBER	CASE DESCRIPTION
11	Production replication team within a Broadway musical company
12	Product development team within a shoe company
13	Metal sculptor
14	Metal sculptor
15	Oil painter
16	Glass artist (makes functional objects, such as goblets)
17	Pottery artist
18	Print maker
19	Metal sculptor
20	Glass sculptor (makes conceptual sculptures)
21	Painter (mixed media)
22	Painter (mixed media)
23	Glass artist
24	Glass artist
25	Jazz musician
26	Classical musician
27	Operations team within an airline
28	Agile software development team within a university
29	Video game development team
30	Video game development team

RESEARCH APPROACH

For those interested in such things, we offer here a description of the details of our research approach.

We employed an inductive, grounded theory, multiphase research design, moving from Phase 1, loosely structured in-depth observation and open-ended interviewing within two cases, to Phase 2, semistructured interviews and observation of a larger number of cases, sampled theoretically along dimensions that emerged from analysis in Phase 1 (Yin 1984; Glasser 1978; Strauss 1987; Eisenhardt 1989; Strauss and Corbin 1998; Miles and Huberman 1994). This book focuses on thirty-five case studies from Phase 2. Although we do not focus on Phase 1, we need to explain briefly its approach, to make clear the overall design of the study and to explain the Phase 2 sampling approach.

PHASE 1—EXPLORING PARALLELS BETWEEN AGILE SOFTWARE DEVELOPMENT AND COLLABORATIVE ARTS PROCESSES

The first phase of this research investigated similarities in the detailed processes and vocabulary in use in what seem like disparate domains of innovative activity: "agile" software development

(Beck 1999; Highsmith 1999) and theatre production. Each of the authors of this book was engaged in research on one of these domains; we noticed the similarities in discussions, at first casual but increasingly serious, then decided to study the matter systematically. We designed Phase 1 to find out if the apparent similarities were real, and, if they were, to explain them.

Most noticeably, each domain relies on "iterative" processes. This means quickly trying things, considering the result, and then trying something else. Software developers called this "prototyping"; theater artists called it "rehearsal," but much other vocabulary was similar (both talked of their processes as "conversations," for example). The relatively recent agile software development movement is, in essence, a rebellion against traditional planning-based software engineering, especially the "software industrial revolution" (Cox 1990) often aspired to by purveyors of that approach, which casts programmers as assembly line workers, not creative contributors (Austin and Devin 2009). While "two ostensibly conflicting approaches . . . [competing] for hegemony" (Boehm and Turner 2003, p. xix) characterized that discussion, we noted that in theater production iterative processes (rehearsal) and planning-based processes (set and costume design) coexist peacefully within the same organization and projects. This led us to focus on theater production for a close look at both kinds of processes and the reasons to employ each. We conducted an in-depth study of a theater company, and, in parallel, also interviewed half a dozen members of agile software development teams.

At a major U.S. regional theater, we initially observed rehearsals and other less iterative activities in progress for periods of several days, to see how processes worked and their outcomes emerged, and to refine our plan for more detailed study. With the help of a research assistant we observed and documented activities throughout an entire five-week rehearsal period for a play; after opening night, we continued to observe consecutive performances, documenting the play's evolution throughout the run. We also conducted open-ended interviews with actors, business managers, designers, directors, dramaturgs, and literary managers. We recorded and transcribed interviews and examined archival sources (such as budgets, strategic plans, and marketing materials). In parallel, we conducted interviews with selected agile software developers.

We analyzed these theater materials using accepted procedures for qualitative data analysis (Eisenhardt 1989; Strauss and Corbin 1998; Miles and Huberman 1994), mining them for recurrent ideas and concepts, categories, and the relationships between them. Curiosity about similarities to agile software development focused our inquiry. We analyzed emerging interpretations and conclusions independently, then subjected them to collective scrutiny. Eventually we arrived at consensus hypotheses about the origins of different process structures. Specifically, we found that two factors, in combination, determined choice of iterative or planning-based process structures:

1. Benefit likely to result from creating original outcomes

2. Cost likely to be incurred in creating original outcomes

The primary purpose of iteration, we realized, was to create an outcome different from previous outcomes. Iterative processes arose most readily, then, under conditions in which original outcomes would be (1) likely to generate ample benefits and (2) likely to incur low costs. We labeled such conditions "innovation-conducive," and contrasted them with conditions in which original outcomes stood little chance of being beneficial, or in which they were prohibitively costly to produce.

Contrasts we observed led us to develop tentative dichotomous scales to summarize the differences we observed. For example, we noted that benefits and costs expected in certain conditions can be high or low, that process structure can be more or less iterative, and that makers can be more or less open to failure and accidents in their work. These scales would become more important and more formalized in Phase 2.

PHASE 2—EXAMINING WORK PRACTICES
IN CONDITIONS CONDUCIVE AND NOT
CONDUCIVE TO INNOVATION

Findings in Phase 1 suggested that management and work practices, including those that concern process structure and accidental innovation, differ according to the degree to which makers work in innovation-conducive conditions. We designed Phase 2 to explore these differences by examining a wide range of making activities.

Sampling Approach

For Phase 2, we sought cases of people and organizations working in conditions we believed would vary in the degree to which original outcomes might be beneficial or costly to produce; that is, we employed "theoretical sampling" (Eisenhardt 1989) along axes of benefit and cost of producing original outcomes. We selected cases on the basis of our understanding of the competitive contexts of particular industries and on our estimates of the cost of iterative work practices in those same contexts. So, for example, we chose a capital-intensive manufacturing case (Case 7) because we believed that originality of outcomes might not be beneficial in that setting, because unplanned variation would be considered a quality problem, and because we believed reconfiguring manufacturing equipment and processes would be costly; this was, we thought, a *low*-benefit, *high*-cost case. We chose a project team in a graphic design firm (Case 5), because we believed that original outcomes would be considered beneficial in that setting (the firm's customers wanted originality), and to try again required only inexpensive changes on a computer screen;

thus, this case was, we thought, a *high*-benefit, *low*-cost case.[1,2] We recruited cases using personal networks and those of our colleagues, and made contact directly, with cold calls or email, or through introductions arranged by colleagues. In five cases (8, 12, 20, 29, and 30), we applied our analysis protocol to trusted secondary sources (such as case studies written by colleagues). You can find a list of our cases, thirty in all, in the previous section of this book.

Although all the people and groups in these cases make things, not all work in conditions conducive to innovation, and not all innovate. In choosing cases, we adopted a definition of innovation, "activity intended to create original, beneficial outcomes," that allowed us to draw from widely ranging domains of activity, across which notions of "benefit" might vary. We drew cases from the arts, design, entertainment, product development, and scientific research. Our definition and approach to sampling are consistent with our interest in principles of innovation that, because they apply across a range of situations, might be considered fundamental.

Fourteen case subjects are individual artists. Like product developers or drug researchers, artists make new things; they make decisions that are based on benefits and costs of producing original outcomes. They work in ways we could easily observe; we could watch the creation of a new metal sculpture from start to finish, unlike creation of a new drug. Our movement back and forth between small-scale (for example, metal sculpture) and large-scale (such as drug development) settings generated rich comparisons, and our observations of the former helped us reach insightful interpretations of the latter. As a bonus, many artists spoke eloquently about why and how they work, and about the role of accident.[3]

It would be wrong to imagine that art cases clustered only with other art cases and business cases clustered only with other business cases on sampling dimensions. For example, the low-benefit, high-cost group contains both capital-intensive manufacturing operations (Case 7) and a team mounting a Broadway musical (Case 11). The Broadway musical team, like the team working in manufacturing, saw their job as using diverse inputs (such as actors) to produce an outcome as near as possible to identical with a specification (the New York production)[4]; the complex machinery that delivered the show's spectacular visual and aural effects made changes costly, as they would be in a manufacturing process. The people in these (L-B, H-C) cases worked in conditions not very conducive to innovation. Cases that focused on people working in conditions conducive to innovation (H-B, L-C) were also mixes of art and business (the H-B, L-C group contains a print maker, Case 18, and an industrial process improvement team, Case 6).

Data-Gathering Protocol

To gather data, we relied on semistructured "template" interviews, observation, and analysis of archival information (mostly documents). We conducted "non-template" interviews to obtain context information about industry, business model, and so on, to help us interpret template interviews and as a check on the consistency of information obtained in those interviews.

To conduct interviews, we followed a protocol designed to start a subject talking in her or his own terms. Using open-ended questions from a prepared interview guide, we introduced topics (including process structure and accident) that had surfaced in Phase 1. Then we probed with follow-up questions, most of them prepared and in the guide. By designing interviews this way, we could be sure of covering a consistent set of topic areas with each person, without precluding other topics that might come up, and without causing them to adopt our language or be influenced by our ideas.

We anchored each interview to a specific example of something that our subject had recently made. We also probed subjects' notions of ideal (not necessarily achievable) ways of working; we aimed to understand both how they did work and how they aspired to work. We videotaped all interviews. After six initial interviews, the research team expanded to six people: two principals, one senior researcher, and three research assistants (two of whom had backgrounds as professional artists). Three researchers (one principal, the senior researcher, and one full-time research assistant) repeatedly screened early interviews to evaluate the interview guide and to refine the interview protocol and guide. This resulted in minor refinement of categories and constructs from Phase 1 and their dichotomous scales.

Analysis Protocol

We used a data-analysis protocol that minimized the possibility of biased evidence selection and ensured that different researchers analyzing the same content would arrive at similar conclusions (reliability among analysts). We revisited interviews as researchers analyzed their content in steps:

1. Watch entire interview, take notes on major concepts. On this pass, we asked researchers to keep broad questions in mind, such as, "What are the most important parts of this process?" and "What is the sequence of activities?"

2. Watch interviews looking for material that corresponds to categories of interest from Phase 1; transcribe, highlight relevant sections, further refine qualitative interpretations.

3. Watch interviews and study transcribed excerpts to arrive at a 1 to 5 coding along the dichotomous scales developed in Phase 1.

Process scope definition was very important in analysis, especially in Step 3 of the protocol. Analysts had to agree on the scope, or they could not code reliably. If one analyst included menu item development at the fast food chain (Case 8) within her scope and the other did not, for example, they would arrive at different interpretations and numerical ratings in Step 3. To facilitate agreement on each process scope, analysts, in conversation with other researchers, constructed a process diagram for each case.

Early in Phase 2 we further refined our dichotomous scales. To refine scales and arrive at language to maximize the reliability of numeric coding, we worked with a practice interview that was not part of our data set. We continued with minor refinements using the first six interviews, always attentive to whether refinements would change the coding of already coded interviews. Though we continued to develop the language of our "coding template" in minor ways throughout the project, (usually to make language for a wider range of making activities), we did most of the refinement in the very early stages. We had a stable coding process by the time we began in earnest on our case analyses.[5] We dropped some scales because we could not make them reliable; we captured only descriptive data in these areas.

Two researchers, never including the researcher who had conducted the interview, analyzed each interview using this procedure. Each analyst had been trained in the procedure using the videotaped practice interview that was not part of our data set.[6] After individual analysts arrived at results, the two compared and discussed results in the presence of a third party. This comparison changed most (but not all) disagreements into agreement; a very few agreements changed to disagreements.[7] The third party ensured that new agreements were arrived at "for good reason" (for example, because one analyst had genuinely shifted from a poor or incorrect interpretation to a better or correct interpretation), not just because of a desire to agree.[8] For cases in which we conducted more than one template interview (ten of the thirty cases), we computed average ratings on the 1 to 5 scales and used those for the final presentation of the case. When the case involved a team, we took care to investigate large differences within a working group.[9] As mentioned, we also used our analysis protocol to assess five already written documents (complete and carefully observed case studies).[10] In other cases we used secondary sources, such as observation and examination of documents, for triangulation. This added to our confidence in the coding procedure.

We assembled results of this process, along with other materials (other diagrams, photos, additional notes, extra materials provided by case subjects), into "case treatments," one for each case. These case treatments typically ran to between 60 and 120 single-spaced pages. "Within-case analysis" of each case, conducted in conference calls (we were a geographically distributed team), led to additions and refinements. Then the team analyzed and compared across cases, using dichotomous scales to suggest contrasts (for example, comparing cases close to 1 with those close to 5) across the sample, and to arrive at general theoretical conclusions (Eisenhardt 1989).

NOTES

1. The company has grown at 30 to 50 percent in recent years. Since the financial crisis began in 2008, the growth has leveled off, but continues to trend in a positive direction.

2. This is our estimate. Vipp doesn't share production cost information.

3. In January of 2008, Apple reported sales of 163 million iPods, up from 100 million in April of 2007.

4. With this move, Walmart reacted to the success of competitor Target, which had introduced a wide range of products under the heading "Design for All," modestly elegant products with higher but still reasonable prices and profit margins higher than Walmart's. See Jacobs 2007.

5. Bianco 2007.

6. Ibid.

7. There are exceptions, of course. By the spring of 2011, the budget for a Broadway musical, *Spider-Man*, had passed $70 million, and the opening had been postponed several times. After about a hundred previews the show was withdrawn for a month so that extensive "improvements" could be made. It finally opened on June 15, 2011.

8. Some people like to distinguish between art and design. One of our colleagues says that art is motivated by self-expression, whereas

design is motivated by a desire to accomplish something for a client. We're open to such distinctions, and find them useful for many purposes. In this book, however, we'll focus on the similarities between art and design objects: structural qualities they share, which we've named with words such as *plot* and *coherence*. The similarities matter more than the differences within the explanations we're unraveling.

9. Telford 1985, p. 13. "Plot, therefore, is the principle and, as it were, the soul of tragedy. . . . " For us, plot is the soul of design.

10. Aristotle is very careful to direct his attention, and ours, not to plays (made by a team and performed for an audience) but to scripts (written by a single artist and read by individuals). He signals this direction of attention by excluding from his discussion two of the qualities he ascribes to tragedies: he calls them spectacle and music (what a spectator sees and what a spectator hears). These are, he says, qualities of production, undertaken by artists other than the poet, and so he leaves them out. He treats his example of making, tragedy, as standing alone, its parts organized on internal principles, and he strongly criticizes poets who take audience desires into consideration. Apply this notion to products you know: you can pick out the ones that were made in response to focus groups or other limited market research.

11. Telford 1985, p. ix and p. 13.

12. See, for example, Peterson and Anand 2004; Becker 1982; Bourdieu 1983; Bourdieu 1985; and DiMaggio 1987.

13. A piece of instrumental music is, for laypersons, a good example of an object that has no ordinary meaning beyond its own completion.

14. See, for example, Austin and Devin 2010.

15. For those of you interested in such things, you can find a more detailed description of our research approach in the section "Research Approach" near the back of this book. Our primary methodological guidelines come from Yin 1984; Glasser 1978; Eisenhardt 1989; Miles and Huberman 1994; and Strauss and Corbin 1998. For an interesting discussion of the place of such research in the development of science, see Deutsch 2011.

16. A version of this quotation has been published previously in Austin and Beyersdorfer 2007, p. 8.

PART 2

1. Examples like this are widely used in education and psychology settings; see, for instance, the "Thurstone Letter Series Completion Test." See Simon and Kotovsky 1963.

2. Banbury and Tremblay 2004. Original reference is to Klaus Conrad, *Die beginnende Schizophrenie. Versuch einer Gestaltanalyse des Wahns* (Stuttgart: Thieme, 1958).

3. Kahneman and Tversky 1982, p. 344.

4. Feller 1968.

5. Conrad 1958; see Hubscher 2007.

6. Fischhoff and Slovic 1980.

7. Gilovich, Vallone, and Tversky 1985.

8. Tversky and Kahneman 1971.

9. Guwande 1988.

10. See Hubscher 2007.

11. For an interesting take on the effects of alphabetic writing on Western culture, see Osborne 2006, especially Chapter 2, "A Torrent of Words."

12. Ellen Dissanayake 2000. See Chapter 1 for photographs of mothers and babies practicing imitation as a way of learning and a source of delight. Professor Dissanayake has influenced us in a big way. Our footnote citations don't do justice to the debt we owe her. Her suggestion, in *What Is Art For?* (1988), that there is a human instinct to "make things special," began our train of thought about the appeal of non-ordinary products, that its mystery might reach deep into human evolution. In her three books (see the bibliography) she makes and supports the assertion that this instinct is part of human biology. We think this helps account for the uncanny power of the products we're reflecting on; there's more to it, in other words, than good business.

13. Telford 1985, p. 6. "For men delight in seeing likenesses because in contemplating them it happens that they are learning and reasoning out what each thing is. . . . "

14. Langer 1953, p. 379. "The import of an art symbol cannot be built up like the meaning of a discourse, but must be seen *in toto* first; that is, the "understanding" of a work of art begins with an intuition

of the whole presented feeling. Contemplation then gradually reveals the complexities of the piece, and of its import." She's talking about *objets d'art*, of course; we extrapolate to apply her observations to non-ordinary business products.

15. "The truths known by intuition are the original premises from which all others are inferred." Mill 2010, p. 1.

16. Psychologists have a precise and elegant way of determining whether a person has "attained" an idea or concept, despite the noise of spurious variation or blurry definitional edges. If the person can sort items that embody the idea (for example, red items) from items that do not embody the concept (that is, not red items), then the person has attained the concept (Simon and Kotovsky 1963).

17. Hamilton 1963, p. 115.

18. See, for example, Miller 2007 or Hassabis, Kumaran, Vann, and Maguire 2007.

19. Berger and Luckmann, 1966. And recall the idea that aesthetic standards are also socially constructed.

20. As in the case of Ellen Dissanayake, our debt to Aristotle cannot be discharged by mere citations. In what follows, readers familiar with *Poetics* will recognize our use of his ideas about making, which he demonstrated in his analysis of tragedy.

21. Poincaré 2003, p. 100.

22. Steinbeck 1937, p. 9.

23. This script is widely available. It's been made into two movies (1939 and 1992), also easy to find.

24. You'd be astonished at their number and variety. For instance, Curly likes to pet his wife, also; he keeps his right hand soft and free of calluses for that purpose by wearing a glove filled with Vaseline.

25. These will differ from those of the original maker. To an old tune, that maker put words that refer maliciously to Queen Mary I of England (Bloody Mary, 1516–1568) and her persecution of Protestants. Today, you aren't likely to get this—we looked it up. A cozy memory of domestic comfort and safety is quite a change from the life or death politics of high treason, even though the song was written long after the events it invokes. (Nobody knows the original source of this very old song.)

PART 3

1. The script by Shakespeare is very well plotted, famously so. The play we saw, made from that script without Shakespeare's help, was not.

2. Aristotle 1941.

3. This tautology comes in very handy, especially for making innovations. Nothing limits imagination more effectively than a preconceived idea about how an emergent thing should turn out. After all, if you can predict it, how new can it be?

4. We quote here from the lectures and conversation of Bernard Beckerman, a famous teacher of dramaturgy. During a seminar Lee attended at Columbia University in about 1975, he asked this question of play scripts, each of them one of a kind; we adopt it for other sorts of unique made things.

5. Beckerman's second question.

6. Remember that memory and imagination use the same machinery in your brain. *Creating* this memory is a task of your imagination.

7. Sequence is of course a time idea. It works for objects and ideas because, after the éclat of intuition, people contemplate things one part or feature at a time.

8. In another *Hamlet* we saw, the actor playing Rosencranz sought to increase his character's magnitude and thus importance by sneaking onstage during Hamlet's soliloquy that begins "Now I am alone . . . ". This had results entirely opposite to those intended: (1) it threw Rosencranz completely out of the play, and (2) it threw the actor completely out of a job. In a really complicated special thing, coherence is a delicate matter, easily upset.

9. In our research, we captured these gestures, and others like them, on video during interviews conducted in the spring of 2006 in Copenhagen, Denmark.

10. Gestures captured on video, spring 2006, Copenhagen, Denmark.

11. Gestures captured on video, spring 2006, Copenhagen, Denmark.

12. See Austin, Devin, and Sullivan, forthcoming.

13. Becque 1913, p. 160.

14. Shakespeare is a good source for learning to recognize the affective significance that resides in anticipation, realization, and closure. For instance, *Romeo and Juliet* is full of rhymed couplets, and when Romeo and Juliet meet, they converse in a sonnet. These materials serve as a suggestive atmosphere that prepares spectators for the larger patterns and their trajectories that plot the story. Learning and responding to Shakespeare's language and plot skills is good practice for thinking about special things and managing the teams that make them.

15. De Vany 2004.

16. Goldman 1983, p. 48.

17. Peirce 1901, paragraph 219.

18. Eikhof and Haunschild 2007, p. 523.

19. An earlier version of this quotation was published in Austin and Beyersdorfer 2007, p. 5.

20. Austin and Beyersdorfer, p. 8.

21. Verganti 2006.

22. An earlier version of this quotation was published in Austin and Beyersdorfer 2006, p. 6.

PART 4

1. Joyce 1939, p. 3.

2. This is a partial number, based on difficult but thorough research; Peter Mahon tells a great story about his efforts to find sales figures, in spite of indifference and downright opposition from publishers and the Joyce estate. See Mahon 2007.

3. "NightLine: The Deep Dive," 1999.

4. MacCormack and D'Angelo 2005.

5. MacCormack and D'Angelo, p. 6.

6. Ebert 1999.

7. The figures are based on data from the Box Office Mojo website (http://boxofficemojo.com/).

8. De Vany 2004, p. 2.

9. The actual communication is probably more like, "You gotta see this; it really grabbed me."

10. India continues to operate as a "production" company that allows e-Types to accept work (and capture revenues) the firm might previously have passed on. But recent reports suggest that work at

India has evolved to include more design activities than originally expected. According to Overgaard, "We have found out that as a company we are still selling attractiveness, a love of design, and a strong opinion on what design should and should not be and do." As a result, India has hired two designers and today has higher "design content" than was originally expected. Cooperation between e-Types and India often works in a very seamless way. "We say that India does not only work with production but with 'design implementation, realization of visual identities, and graphic production'," says Overgaard.

11. An earlier version of this quotation was published in Austin and Shifrin 2007, p. 3.

12. See Caves 2000; and Florida 2002.

13. Davis and Scase 2000.

14. Sutton 2001; also Florida 2002.

15. The guys who make commercials at the ad agency refer to the indispensable actors as "the talent," a commodity they're lumbered with and wish they could do without.

16. Asperger's Syndrome has less pronounced symptoms than many forms of autism and is often diagnosed at more advanced ages.

17. National Autistic Society 2012a.

18. National Autistic Society 2012b.

19. Streaming video of this session is available on the Web; see University of Washington Television, 2006.

20. De Vany 2004. *The Sixth Sense*, which opened on 2,161 screens, a sign of producer confidence, achieved both these nominations, but won neither award.

21. De Vany 2004, p. 23.

22. Mass Animation Faccbook page, http://www.facebook.com/massanimation.

23. As of 2008.

24. They did this in partnership with Reel FX and Gentle Giant; Robertson 2009.

25. Robertson 2009.

PART 5

1. "I was so bad," he said later, "I thought I'd go study dentistry" (Davis's father was a dentist). Miles Davis, in an interview with Steve

Rowland, *Miles Davis Radio Project*, part 2 of 7, American Public Radio, quoted in Kahn 2001, p. 28.

2. Cannonball Adderley, quoted in Gitler 1959, p. 203; also in Kahn, p. 40.

3. Robert Palmer, from the liner notes of the 1997 reissue of the album.

4. See Evans, "Liner Notes" for the full essay.

5. From the album's original liner notes.

6. Of course we can't predict any one listener's response. But the sales figures for *Kind of Blue* in the more than fifty years of its life give us confidence in supposing that this reaction to this music is no longer uncommon.

7. We mentioned this in Part 1, and cited "Not Just a Pretty Face" (Austin and Devin 2010). In it we discuss in detail the forces of change at work and speculate on their results.

RESEARCH APPROACH

1. After gathering data, we discovered that we had been wrong in our ideas about some cases, that benefit or cost of original outcomes was higher or lower than expected. In Case 7, for example, we were largely correct about cost, but not as correct about the benefits of originality (as will become apparent later). Because we anticipated making at least a few such errors, however, we chose enough cases to span extremes of all high and low benefit and cost combinations; and despite some errors in our forecasts, our sample did in the end include all possible combinations.

2. When we selected cases we took some care to define the specific process scope. Differences in process scope could, by changing the focus of a case, cause changes in estimates and assessment of the benefits and costs of originality. For example, in Case 8 we focused on fast food making and delivery in a restaurant, a scope that did not include the development of new menu items (new product development); a case that focused on new product development for the same company would, no doubt, have resulted in a different mix of benefits and costs.

3. By comparison, some business subjects were reserved on the subject of accident, because (as some explained) words such as *accident*, *mistake*, and *failure* have strong negative connotations within common business ways of thinking.

4. Said the show director, "I'm not doing this to find a new and better way to do [the show]. . . . Our mandate is . . . to re-create the brand as faithfully as we possibly can. . . . An audience should feel if they see [the show] in São Paulo that it's as good, and exactly the same as, [the show] in London or New York."

5. Working iteratively, we ultimately developed thirteen versions of the "coding template" that we used in analysis. Versions 1 through 9, which accomplished the bulk of the scale-refinement process, resulted from work with the practice interview not part of our data set. Versions 10 and 11 involved small changes during the analysis of the first six cases. Versions 12 and 13 involved minor changes, mainly to adapt the interview to include more complex making situations. For example, we adjusted wording to include work in the pharmaceuticals industry when we began to analyze our first pharma case. The changes from Version 9 to Version 13 were not substantive in terms of definitions, but mostly involved adjustments to more inclusive language. All coding used template Versions 11 or higher. We also looped back to early interviews to make sure that the process used to analyze them was consistent with the process for later interviews.

6. When we added an analyst relatively late in the project, we also used early, already reliably coded interviews to train her. These *were* in our data set, but by this time the coding process had stabilized, and the coding of these interviews (the ones used in training) was already a settled matter. We used a total of three coding analysts throughout the project.

7. In the very rare cases when a disagreement persisted, we averaged the ratings. We never, however, averaged ratings of different valence (that is, for example, 1 and 4). Differences of valence typically resulted from different assumptions (for example, in process scope) and were handled in discussions between researchers; none survived those discussions for scales we retained as reliable. Too frequent valence differences in coding caused us to drop some scales.

8. Disagreement because of poor or incorrect interpretation usually arose from difficulties in interpreting how a scale should apply to a domain of making activity we had not analyzed before. For example, before we began analysis of pharma cases, we had not had much practice in applying concepts represented in our analysis protocol to

the specifics of pharma activities. Once in a while, in discussing coding of such new situations, analysts learned how existing language should apply to the new context; when this happened, it sometimes caused an analyst to change interpretation and, occasionally, scale coding.

9. There were very few examples of this. Where it did occur, as in one design firm, it was the result of an active disagreement about the future direction of the firm and the outlier subject was at odds with others within the firm over this issue. In one other instance, the outlier was relatively new to the firm and thus not yet fully familiar with its operating context. We opted to exclude the outliers from averages.

10. In two of these cases, we had access to the authors of the written documents that we content-analyzed; thus we were able to check our interpretations with them. Our analysis protocol proved quite capable of dealing with varied content sources. Our semistructured template interviews had this advantage over secondary sources: they covered the issues more comprehensively. Even detailed secondary sources were more likely to leave gaps in our analysis. But the three secondary source cases we included gave us nicely complete results.

BIBLIOGRAPHY

PERIODICALS

Austin, Robert D., and Lee Devin. "Not Just a Pretty Face: Economic Drivers Behind the Arts-in-Business Movement." *Journal of Business Strategy* 31, no. 4 (2010): 59–69.

———. "Research Commentary: Weighing the Benefits and Costs of Flexibility in Making Software: Toward a Contingency Theory of the Determinants of Development Process Design." *Information Systems Research* 20, no. 3 (2009): 462–477.

Austin, Robert D., Lee Devin, and Erin Sullivan. "Accidental Innovation: Supporting Valuable Unpredictability in Creative Process." *Organization Science*, forthcoming.

Bianco, Anthony. "Wal-Mart's Mid-Life Crisis." *Business Week*, April 30, 2007.

Bourdieu, Pierre. "The Field of Cultural Production or the Economic World Reversed." *Poetics* 12 (1983): 311–356.

———. "The Market of Symbolic Goods." *Poetics* 14 (1985): 13–44.

Cox, Brad J. "Planning the Software Industrial Revolution." *IEEE Software* 7, no. 6 (1990): 25–33.

DiMaggio, Paul. "Classification in Art." *American Sociological Review* 52 (1987): 440–455.

Eikhof, Doris Ruth, and Axel Haunschild. "For Art's Sake! Artistic and Economic Logics in Creative Production." *Journal of Organizational Behavior* 28 (2007): 523.

Eisenhardt, Kathleen M. "Building Theories from Case Study Research." *The Academy of Management Review* 14, no. 4 (October 1989): 532–550.

Gilovich, Thomas, Robert Vallone, and Amos Tversky. "The Hot Hand in Basketball: On the Misperception of Random Sequences." *Journal of Personality and Social Psychology* 17 (1985): 295–314.

Gitler, Ira. "Listening to Miles." *Jazz Quarterly*, Summer 1959, 203.

Guwande, Atul. "The Cancer Cluster Myth." *The New Yorker*, February 8, 1988, 34–37.

Hassabis, Demis, Dharshan Kumaran, Seralynne D. Vann, and Eleanor A. Maguire. "Patients with Hippocampal Amnesia Cannot Imagine New Experiences." *Proceedings of the National Academy of Sciences* 104, no. 5 (January 30, 2007): 1726–1731.

MacCormack, Alan, and Enrico D'Angelo. "Activision: The *Kelly Slater's Pro Surfer* Project." HBS case #605-020, 2005.

Mahon, Peter. "Buying and Selling *Finnegans Wake*." *James Joyce Quarterly* 44, no. 4 (Summer 2007): 800–806.

Miller, Greg. "A Surprising Connection Between Memory and Imagination." *Science* 315, no. 5810 (January 19, 2007): 312.

Peterson, Richard A., and N. Anand. "The Production of Culture Perspective." *Annual Review of Sociology* 30 (2004): 311–334.

Simon, Herbert A., and Kenneth Kotovsky. "Human Acquisition of Concepts for Sequential Patterns." *Psychological Review* 70, no, 6 (November 1963): 534–546.

Sutton, Robert. "The Weird Rules of Creativity." *Harvard Business Review* 79 (2001): 94–103.

Tversky, Amos, and Daniel Kahneman. "Belief in the Law of Small Numbers." *Psychological Bulletin* 76 (1971): 105–110.

Verganti, Roberto. "Innovating Through Design." *Harvard Business Review* 84, no. 12 (December 2006): 114–122.

INTERNET

Amid. "Mass Animation or Mass Exploitation?" Cartoon Brew, August 22, 2008. http://www.cartoonbrew.com/ideas-commentary/mass-animation-or-mass-exploitation.html.

Box Office Mojo. http://boxofficemojo.com/.

Ebert, Roger. "The Blair Witch Project." rogerebert.com, July 16, 1999. http://rogerebert.suntimes.com/apps/pbcs.dll/article?AID=/ 19990716/REVIEWS/907160301/1023.

Evans, Bill. Liner notes for *Kind of Blue*. The Bill Evans Webpages. http://www.billevanswebpages.com/kindblue.html; accessed January 31, 2012.

Hubscher, Sandra. "Apophenia: Definition and Analysis." *Digital Bits Skeptic*, November 4, 2007. http://www.dbskeptic.com/2007/11/04/ apophenia-definition-and-analysis.

Jacobs, Daniel. "Wal-Mart's Upscale Move into Target Territory." *International Business Times*, August 21, 2006. http://www.ibtimes.com/ articles/20060821/walmart-target-retail-upscale-competition.htm.

Mass Animation Facebook page. http://www.facebook.com/ massanimation; accessed January 31, 2012.

National Autistic Society. "What Is Autism?" The National Autistic Society, January 4, 2012a. http://www.autism.org.uk/about-autism/ autism-and-asperger-syndrome-an-introduction/what-is-autism.aspx.

National Autistic Society. "Autism and Asperger Syndrome: Some Facts and Statistics." The National Austistic Society, January 4, 2012b. http://www.autism.org.uk/about-autism/some-facts-and -statistics.aspx.

Palmer, Robert. "Liner Notes." *Kind of Blue*, Sony Music Entertainment/Columbia Records, 1997 reissue. http://www.billevansweb pages.com/kindblue.html.

Robertson, Barbara. "Crowding: The First CG Short Film Created via Facebook by Animators Around the World Lands on the Big Screen." *Computer Graphics World*, November 2009. http:// digital.copcomm.com/title/3812.

University of Washington Television, "Organizational Dilemma of Stewards and Creators," July 10, 2006. http://www.uwtv.org/ programs/displayevent.aspx?rID=4858.

BOOKS, CASES, AND ART WORKS

Aristotle. *Physics*, Book II, Chapter 3. In *The Basic Works of Aristotle*, edited by Richard McKeon, 240, ff. New York: Random House, 1941.

Austin, Robert D., and Daniela Beyersdorfer. *Vipp A/S*. Boston: Harvard Business School Publishing, 2006.

———. *Bang & Olufsen: Design Driven Innovation*. Boston: Harvard Business School Publishing, 2007.

Austin, Robert D., and Deborah Shifrin. *Ascent Media Group (A)*. Boston: Harvard Business School Publishing, 2007.

Banbury, Simon, and Sebastien Tremblay, eds. *A Cognitive Approach to Situation Awareness: Theory and Application*, 1st ed. Burlington, VT: Ashgate, 2004.

Beck, Kent. *Extreme Programming Explained: Embrace Change*. Boston: Addison-Wesley, 1999.

Becker, Howard. *Art Worlds*. Berkeley: University of California Press, 1982.

Becque, Henry. *Three Plays by Henry Becque,* translated by Freeman Tilden. New York: Mitchell Kennerly, 1913.

Berger, P., and T. Luckmann. *The Social Construction of Reality: A Treatise on the Sociology of Knowledge*. London: Penguin University Books, 1966.

Boehm, B., and Richard Turner. *Balancing Agility and Discipline: A Guide for the Perplexed*. Boston: Addison-Wesley Professional, 2003.

Cassidy, Eva. *Songbird*, Blix Street Records, 1998.

Caves, Richard E. *Creative Industries: Contracts Between Arts and Commerce*. Cambridge, MA: Harvard University Press, 2000.

Conrad, Klaus. *Die beginnende Schizophrenie. Versuch einer Gestaltanalyse des Wahns*. Stuttgart: Thieme, 1958.

Davis, Howard, and Richard Scase. *Managing Creativity: The Dynamics of Work and Organization*. Buckingham and Philadelphia: Open University Press, 2000.

Davis, Mile. *Kind of Blue*. Columbia: Legacy; remastered, 1997.

Deutsch, David. *The Beginning of Infinity: Explanations That Transform the World*. New York: Viking, 2011.

De Vany, Arthur. *Hollywood Economics: How Extreme Uncertainty Shapes the Film Industry*. London: Routledge, 2004.

Dissanayake, Ellen. *What Is Art For?* Seattle: University of Washington Press, 1988.

———. *Homo Aestheticus: Where Art Comes From and Why*. New York: The Free Press, 1992.

———. *Art and Intimacy: How the Arts Began*. Seattle: University of Washington Press, 2000.

Florida, Richard. *The Rise of the Creative Class: And How It's Transforming Work, Leisure, Community, and Everyday Life.* New York: Basic Books, 2002.

Feller, William. *An Introduction to Probability Theory and Its Application.* Hoboken, NJ: John Wiley & Sons, 1968.

Fischhoff, B., and P. Slovic. "A Little Learning: Confidence in Multi-Cue Judgment Tasks." In *Attention and Performance VIII*, edited by R. Nickerson. Hillsdale, NJ: Erlbaum, 1980.

Glasser, B. G. *Theoretical Sensitivity: Advances in the Methodology of Grounded Theory,* Mills, CA: Sociology Press, 1978.

Goldman, William. *Adventures in the Screen Trade.* New York: Warner Books, 1983.

Hamilton, Edith. *Three Greek Plays.* New York: W. W. Norton, 1963.

Highsmith, James A. III. *Adaptive Software Development: A Collaborative Approach to Managing Complex Systems.* New York: Dorset House Publishing, 1999.

Joyce, James. *Finnegans Wake.* New York: Penguin Books, 1939.

Kahn, Ashley. *Kind of Blue: The Making of the Miles Davis Masterpiece.* Cambridge, MA: Da Capo Press, 2001.

Kahneman, Daniel, and Amos Tversky. "On the Psychology of Prediction," in *Judgment Under Uncertainty: Heuristics and Biases*, edited by Kahneman, Daniel, Paul Slovic, and Amos Tversky. Cambridge, UK: Cambridge University Press, 1982.

Kahneman, Daniel, Paul Slovic, and Amos Tversky, eds. *Judgment Under Uncertainty: Heuristics and Biases,* Cambridge, UK: Cambridge University Press, 1982.

Langer, Susanne K. *Feeling and Form: A Theory of Art.* New York: Charles Scribner's Sons, 1953.

Meyer, Leonard B. *Emotion and Meaning in Music.* Chicago: University of Chicago Press, 1956.

Miles, M., and A. M. Huberman, *Qualitative Data Analysis.* Thousand Oaks, CA: Sage, 1994.

Mill, John S. *A System of Logic, Ratiocinative and Inductive.* Charlestown, NC: Nabu Press, 2010.

Nickerson, R. S., ed. *Attention and Performance VIII.* Hillsdale, NJ: Erlbaum, 1980.

"NightLine: The Deep Dive." ABC News, July 13, 1999.

Osborne, Roger. *Civilization: A New History of the Western World.* New York: Pegasus Books, 2006.

Peirce, Charles Sanders. "On the Logic of Drawing History from Ancient Documents, Especially from Testimonies," in *The Essential Peirce: Selected Philosophical Writings*, (Vol. 2, 1893–1913, pp. 75–114), edited by Houser, N., J. R. Eller, A. C. Lewis, A. D. Tienne, C. L. Clark, and D. B. Davis. Bloomington: Indiana Uniersity Press, 1998 (original published in 1901).

Poincaré, Henri. *Science and Method*, translated by Francis Maitland. Mineola, NY: Dover, 2003.

Steinbeck, John. *Of Mice and Men.* New York: Dramatists Play Service, 1937.

Strauss, A. *Qualitative Analysis for Social Scientists.* Cambridge, UK: Cambridge University Press, 1987.

Strauss, A., and J. Corbin. *Basics of Qualitative Research: Techniques and Procedures for Developing Grounded Theory*, 2nd Ed. Thousand Oaks, CA: Sage, 1998.

Telford, Kenneth. *Aristotle's* Poetics: *Translation and Analysis.* Lanham, MD, and London: University Press of America, 1985.

Yin, R. K., *Case Study Research: Design and Methods.* Beverly Hills, CA: Sage, 1984.

INDEX